THE GREAT UNIVERSAL STUDIOS ORLANDO SCAVENGER HUNT

A DETAILED PATH THROUGH
UNIVERSAL STUDIOS FLORIDA AND
UNIVERSAL'S ISLANDS OF ADVENTURE

CATHERINE F. OLEN

The Great Universal Studios Orlando Scavenger Hunt
A Detailed Path through Universal Studios Florida and Islands of Adventure

© 2020 Catherine Olen

All Rights Reserved. No Portion of this book may be reproduced, stored in a retrieval system, or transmitted in any form or by any means – electronic, mechanical, photocopy, recording, scanning or other – except for brief quotations in critical reviews or articles, without the prior written permission of the publisher. Subject to permission under section 107 and/or 108 of the 1976 United States Copyright act. Requests for permission should be addressed to the publisher wwww.mousehangover.com. 949-234-7332

First paperback edition April 2020

ISBN 978-1-64822-002-9 (paperback)
ISBN 978-1-64822-003-6 (eBook)

Published by Mouse Hangover
www.Mousehangover.com

Please note: Every effort has been made to ensure the accuracy of information throughout this book. The information is believed to be accurate at the time of printing. The publish and author are not responsible for errors or omissions, for changes to details or the consequences of the readers reliance to the information provided.
Attraction closures or updates are not the responsibility of the publisher or author and cannot be guaranteed at the time of use of this book.

Readers are welcome to contact the publisher for comments, updates or questions.

About the Author

Catherine Olen has been visiting Universal Studios theme parks since she was a small child. Olen fell in love with the parks built through the imagination of founder Carl Laemmle and became an annual passholder in 1991 and has held an annual pass ever since.

Olen first traveled to Universal Studios Orlando at the age of thirty, immediately falling in love with the Florida parks. She has traveled to the Universal Studios Orlando theme parks each year since and now travels to Orlando several times a year to revel in the new attractions as well as the classic favorites.

Olen now shares her love of all things Universal in *The Great Universal Studios Orlando Scavenger Hunt*.

Come Check Us Out

Check out new books, video and news at

www.Mousehangover.com
Subscribe to Mouse Hangover
Instagram - @TheMouseHangover
Twitter - @Mousehangover
Facebook - @Mousehangover
@WDWScavengerHunt

YouTube – Mouse Hangover

Other books:

The Great Disneyland Scavenger Hunt
The Great Universal Studios Hollywood Scavenger Hunt
The Great Walt Disney World Scavenger Hunt

Dedication

I dedicate this book to every person that walks through the gates of Universal Studios. It is not enough to go to a dark theater and watch movies. You want to experience the stories for yourselves. I hope this book enhances your experiences and brightens your day.

To every person in my life that encouraged me to finish this book, thank you for your unending belief and help in more ways than I can enumerate.

Lastly, my thanks to the hundreds of people working at Universal Studios and Islands of Adventure, you are the backbone of the theme parks and I thank you for making my visits special each and every time I stand in the parks.

Contents

Introduction xi

Universal Studios 1
  Production Central 1
    Shrek 4-D 1
    Despicable Me Minion Mayhem 5
    Universal Studios Classic Monster's Cafe 8
    Transformers™ The Ride-3D 9
  New York Street 13
    Race Through New York Starring Jimmy Fallon ... 14
    The Revenge of the Mummy 17
  San Francisco 24
    Richter's Burger Co. 26
    Fast & Furious: Supercharged 26
  The Wizarding World of Harry Potter™ -
  Diagon Alley™ 32
    Knight Bus 32
    Hogwarts™ Express – King's Cross Station 33
    Quality Quidditch™ Supplies 37
    Weasleys' Wizard Wheezes 37
    Gringotts™ Money Exchange 41
    The Leaky Cauldron 42
    Flourish and Blotts Booksellers 43
    Madam Malkin's Robes for All Occasions 45
    Mr. Mulpeppers Apothecary 45
    Florean Fortescue's Ice Cream Parlor 46
    Harry Potter and the Escape from Gringotts™ 46
    Ollivanders™ 49

Magical Menagerie	51
Knockturn Alley	53
Borgin and Burkes™	55
World Expo	58
Men in Black™: Alien Attack	58
Springfield: Home of the Simpsons	61
Fast Food Blvd	62
Moe's Tavern	64
The Kwik-E-Mart	66
Kang and Kodos' Twirl 'N' Hurl	68
The Simpson's Ride	69
Woody Woodpecker's KidZone	75
SpongeBob StorePants	75
E.T. Adventure	76
Fievel's Playland	78
Woody Woodpecker's Nuthouse Coaster	80
Curious George Goes to Town	81
Barney's Backyard	83
Hollywood	84
Universal Orlando's Horror Make-up Show	85
Mel's Diner	87
Schwab's Drug Store	88
Universal's Islands of Adventure	91
Introduction	93
Port of Entry	95
Confisco Grill	98
Marvel Super Hero Island	100
The Incredible Hulk Coaster	101
Doctor Doom's Fearfall	104
The Amazing Adventures of Spiderman™	105
Toon Lagoon	111
Blondies: Home of the Dagwood	113
Dudley Do-Right's Ripsaw Falls™	114

> Comic Strip Café 117
> Popeye and Bluto's Bilge-Rat Barges 118

Skull Island: Reign of Kong 124
Jurassic Park... 128
> Jurassic Park River Adventure............................. 128
> Jurassic Park Discovery Center 129
> Camp Jurassic 131

The Wizarding World of Harry Potter™ - Hogsmeade.. 132
> Honeydukes™ 133
> Three Broomsticks™ 134
> Hog's Head™ Pub 135
> Dervish and Banges™ 137
> Owl Post 138
> Gladrags Wizardwear 139
> Scrivenshaft's Finest Parchment, Ink and Quills . 140
> Madam Puddifoot's 140
> Ceridwen's Cauldron 141
> Tomes and Scrolls Specialist Bookshop.............. 141
> Flight of the Hippogriff™ 142
> Bonus question 143
> Ollivanders™ 143
> Harry Potter and the Forbidden Journey™ 144

The Lost Continent.. 151
> Poseidon's Fury: Escape from the Lost City 152

Seuss Landing 156
> Mulberry Street Store, Gizmo's, Gadgets, Goodies Galore 157
> The High in the Sky Seuss Trolley Train Ride!.... 158
> Dr. Seuss All the Books You Can Read 160
> The Cat in the Hat 162
> One Fish, Two Fish, Red Fish, Blue Fish 164
> If I Ran the Zoo.. 165

Answer Key 169

Introduction

Opening summer of 1990, Universal Studios Florida has brought guests a variety of shows and attractions to demonstrated every aspects of the film industry. The Murder She Wrote and Alfred Hitchcock Art of Movie Making shows brought guests closer to their favorite television series and classic movies.

The E.T. Adventure put guests right in the middle of the action of their favorite science fiction film from the 1980's.

Soon, the park gave way to new thrills like the Terminator 2: 3 D and TWISTER Ride it Out attractions. These new shows brought the latest special effect technology to the theme park while continuing the tradition of putting the guests right in the action.

At the end of the millennium, Universal brought a whole new theme park with Universal's Islands of Adventure. Like its predecessor, Islands of Adventure offered new rides and shows starting with Seuss Landing, Cartoon Lagoon, Jurassic Park and the Lost Continent. Soon, the theme parks were growing with attractions based on your favorite Marvel and Harry Potter stories. These new theme park area drawing guests from all over the world to the Universal Orlando resort.

Catherine F. Olen

My first introduction to Universal Studios Florida was in 2004, when I came upon the massive archway and entered the theme park to encounter TWISTER Ride it Out, Shrek 4D and Revenge of the Mummy. Traveling between the two parks, I was incredibly excited about the 2010 addition of the Wizarding World of Harry Potter™. Walking through Hogsmeade™ brought the sensation of walking right into these enchanting films.

Throughout the years, Universal Studios Orlando has outdone themselves with biggest and better attractions. The years to come bring new and exciting changes for guests of all ages.

How to use this book:

Your Universal trivia is broken down into three categories

- One star – Easier questions – Good for families with small children or first-time guests
- Two stars – Challenging questions – For returning guests and those with more time
- Three stars – Expert questions – For those looking for a real challenge or park experts

All of the questions found in this book have been verified by several Universal enthusiasts, but I am aware that the décor of Universal Studios Orlando changes regularly. If there are changes, you can visit www.MouseHangover.com for current updates. If you have come across a change prior to website updates, please email so the changes can be noted.

I hope you find your way through the Universal Studios Orlando theme parks with new eyes and enjoy your hunt for the details every guest can experience.

Note: All content is subject to change without notice. Ride closures, construction, or overlays for the Halloween and

Christmas holidays may alter the content temporarily due to park-wide decorations.

Trademarks:

This book uses Universal Studios copy-righted characters, registered trademarks, marks, and registered marks of NBC Universal. J.K. Rowling copy righted characters, registered trademarks, marks and registered marks. Living Books owned characters including Dr. Seuss characters, registered trademarks, marks and registered marks. Disney owned characters, registered trademarks, marks and registered marks. The Simpsons, a registered trademark of 20th Century Fox created by Matt Groening.

All reference to celebrity names, trademarks, marks and registers marks are the property of the governing body, Mousehangover.com is in no way affiliated with these entities.

All references to these properties are made solely for editorial purposes. Neither the author nor the publisher makes any commercial claim to their use, and neither is affiliated with Universal Studios or NBC in any way.

Production Central

Enter the sound stages of Production Central as you rub elbows with the biggest stars of today's film and television productions.

Go on an adventure with Shrek and Donkey, become a minion with your favorite bad guy Gru or select your own soundtrack for the wildest roller coaster you can ever imagine. Along the way, grab a bite with the classic film monsters or get your picture taken with cartoon characters come to life.

Shrek 4-D

1. ★ As you enter the queue for Shrek 4-D, Read the signs above you. One sign is for humans, the other is for what type of creatures?
   a. Imaginary
   b. Flying
   c. Fairy tale
   d. Royal

2. ★★ Find the rules for fairytale creatures posted at the entrance of the queue. Individuals talking during the presentation will receive a special V.I.P. demonstration of what?
   a. The strangler
   b. The fire pool
   c. Tilly's house of pain
   d. The crusher

3. ★★ According to the rules for fairytale creatures, all fairytale creatures are required to declare what part of the Griffin?
   a. Toenails
   b. Spleen
   c. Kneecaps
   d. Eyes

4. ★ As you spend your time in line before entering the torture chamber, read some of the wanted posters. According to the wanted poster for Shrek, what does the term "questioning" mean?
   a. Torture
   b. Questioning
   c. Drowning
   d. Starving

5. ★ Find the stroller parking sign in front of the Shrek attraction, what section are you parked in?
   a. Arthur
   b. Lancelot
   c. Percival
   d. Lamorak

6. ★★ Read the notices on the wall as you walk through the queue. At Foe's Village Tavern, you can watch the game on a 32 inch what?
   a. Flat screen television
   b. Glass slipper
   c. Hollow log
   d. Magic mirror

7. ★★ What is the name of the lost fire breathing dragon according to the notice?
   a. Hot stuff
   b. Snuffy
   c. Mr. Sniffles
   d. Mrs. Donkey

8. ★★★ Stop for a moment to read *The Medieval Times*, what production do the three blind mice give three thumbs up to?
   a. *Cat on a Hot Tin Roof*
   b. *Of Mice and Men*
   c. *The Cat in the Hat*
   d. *The Mouse that Roared*

The Great Universal Studios Orlando Scavenger Hunt

9. ★★★ According to the weather report, today will be mild to partly what?
   a. Pixie
   b. Cloudy
   c. Enchanted
   d. Magical

10. ★ As you find the cement block with the footprints of the Shrek characters, which of these is *not* one of the character footprints you see?
    a. Fiona
    b. Donkey
    c. Dragon
    d. Pinocchio

11. ★★ Read the notice for the Fairytale Survivors support group. Pinocchio lost 20 pounds in what period of time?
    a. 6 months
    b. 11 seconds
    c. 30 days
    d. 8 years

12. ★★ What is the address for Sir Crazy Ernie's discount sporting goods?
    a. 1313 Mockingbird Lane
    b. 1453 Candyland
    c. 7 Candy Cane Lane
    d. 2001 Far away

13. ★★ According to the poster for Villain's Tavern, what is the 3-4 a.m. hour for?
    a. Drunkenly call old girlfriends' hour
    b. Happy hour
    c. Sleepy hour
    d. Dopey hour

14. ★★ As you take your seat in the theater and the show begins, you will see Shrek and Donkey go through Gingy's house, what does he tell them it cost him? O2RRF
    a. A lot of candy
    b. A lot of money
    c. A lot of dough
    d. A lot of cookies

15. ★★★ As Shrek and donkey walk through the cemetery, what do the markers on the open graves read?
    a. Vacancy
    b. Loading zone
    c. The end
    d. Coming soon

16. ★ How are Shrek, Fiona, Donkey and Felonius saved from the falls?
    a. Fairies
    b. Dragon
    c. Witches broomstick
    d. Magic carpet

17. ★★ As you exit the Shrek 4-D attraction, spend some time in the gift shop before you move on. What sort of creature is on duty at the pool according to the notice inside the shop?
    a. Dragon
    b. Centaur
    c. Crocodile
    d. Donkey

18. ★ Find Ye Map Quest. Where are you according to the map?
    a. Honeymoon Hotel
    b. Elf Spa
    c. Fairy Falls
    d. Death Canyon

19. ★★ Along route 305 you will find what kind of bridge on Ye Map Quest?
    a. Ogre bridge
    b. Troll bridge
    c. Billy goat bridge
    d. Pixie bridge

20. ★★ Find the posted check out times within the shop. At what time do the gnomes check out?
    a. When people stop believing
    b. 11 am sharp!
    c. Whenever you feel like it
    d. Spring time!

> **Did you know?**
> Watch the mirror behind the counter. Periodically you will see the mirror come to life.

Despicable Me Minion Mayhem

21. ★★ As you enter the queue for Despicable Me Minion Mayhem, stop for a moment at the minion blueprint. How tall are minions?
    a. 2 feet
    b. 4 feet
    c. 5 feet
    d. 3 feet

22. ★★ What sort of brain do Minions have according to their blue prints?
    a. Peanut
    b. Super
    c. Teensy
    d. Legendary

> **Did you know?**
>
> As you enter the first room of Gru's house, look at the shelves around you. You will find the helmet Gru made from a cardboard box, the macaroni prototype of his rocket and his original drawing of the rocket he showed his mother in the first *Despicable Me* movie.

23. ★★★ As you read Gru's family tree, what is the name of the husband at the top of the chart?
    a. Leopold
    b. François
    c. Gru
    d. Lawrence

24. ★ What is Gru's given name according to this chart?
    a. Gru
    b. Theodore
    c. Felonius
    d. Felton

25. ★★★ As you look over Gru's family tree, what sort of creature is married to Yolanda?
    a. Frankenstein monster
    b. Vampire
    c. Werewolf
    d. Mummy

26. ★★★ Find the portrait of Gru surrounded by minions. How many minions or parts of minions do you see in this picture?
    a. 31
    b. 41
    c. 51
    d. 62

27. ★★ As you look around the room, which of these is not one of the animals mounted on the wall?
    a. Bird
    b. Lion
    c. Mouse
    d. Cat

Bonus Question:

28. ★ Which of these is *not* one of the names of Gru's daughters?
    a. Edith
    b. Agnes
    c. Margot
    d. Octavia

29. ★ Find the piranha mounted on the wall, what adorns the piece of cloth in its teeth?
    a. Hearts
    b. Happy faces
    c. Flowers
    d. Teddy bears

30. ★ As you begin the interview process with Gru and the girls come into the room, what object does Edith hold up and call her evil clown?
    a. Unicorn
    b. Teddy bear
    c. Fashion doll
    d. Sock puppet

31. ★★ How long will the written exam take to complete according to Gru?
    a. 3 days
    b. 3 hours
    c. 3 weeks
    d. 3 minutes

32. ★★ The goggles you have will last five times longer than what?

a.	A package of Twinkies	c.	Cher
b.	Cockroaches	d.	The person wearing them

33. ★★ As the minion eats Jalapeno dip, what is in the framed picture in the background?
    a. A fork
    b. Gru's portrait
    c. Flower vase
    d. Minions

34. ★★ As Gru begins your interview, you will see a minion come to him with blue prints. When the minion hands Gru the plans, what does Gru tell him they need more of?
    a. Gun powder
    b. Freeze rays
    c. Explosions
    d. Dynamite

35. ★ What is the scent of the fart gun Gru shoots at you in the pre-boarding room?
    a. Fart
    b. Pineapple
    c. Banana
    d. Rotten fruit

36. ★ As you begin minion training, you will jump over what object in the obstacle course?
    a. A banana
    b. A cactus
    c. A bomb
    d. A Fart gun

37. ★ As you continue running the obstacle course, what are you and the other minions being hit with?
    a. Swings
    b. Hammer
    c. Fly swatter
    d. Glove

38. ★ What color is the bow on Gru's present from the girls?
    a. Yellow
    b. Red
    c. Blue
    d. Green

39. ★★ What is unusual about the recycle area of Gru's lab?
    a. Under water
    b. It's on the moon
    c. High frequency
    d. Anti-gravity

40. ★ What is inside the present Agnes hands to Gru for their anniversary?
    a. Minion doll
    b. Unicorn toy
    c. Gru doll
    d. Sleepy kitty book

> **Did you know?**
> As you exit the Despicable Me Minion Mayhem attraction, stop at the cross walk. You will see this is actually a Minion crossing.

Universal Studios Classic Monster's Cafe

41. ★ As you approach the Monster Café on your right, take a look at the monsters adorning the top of the quick service. Which of these is *not* one of the monsters you see?
    a. Frankenstein monster
    b. Dracula
    c. Werewolf
    d. Creature from the Black Lagoon

42. ★ Find the extreme cold thermometer on the quick service building. How cold is the beverage temperature today?
    a. Spine chilling
    b. Soul chilling
    c. Bone chilling
    d. Thirst chilling

> **Did you know?**
> Walk to the entrance of Monster Café and you will find an electric chair to pose for pictures. Don't miss this lesser known photo opportunity.

The Great Universal Studios Orlando Scavenger Hunt

43. ★★ As you explore the interior of Monster's Café, find the sign for the field expedition. What year is the season on the sign?
    a. 1926
    b. 1931
    c. 1936
    d. 1921

> **Did you know?**
> If you look at the painting of Boris Karloff from the classic film *The Mummy*, you will see around him hieroglyphics. If you look closely, these symbols are food items and eating utensils.

44. ★★ Look above you around Monster's Café and you will see director's chairs with the names of the different movie monsters. What is unique about the chair for Dracula?
    a. It's upside down
    b. It's furry
    c. It's wrapped in bandages
    d. It's covered in seaweed

Bonus Question:

45. ★★★ Find the painting for The Bride of Frankenstein. What famous actress played this iconic role?
    a. Eartha Kitt
    b. Elizabeth Montgomery
    c. Elsa Lanchester
    d. Edith Head

Transformers™ The Ride-3D

46. ★★★ As you approach the entrance for Transformers, The Ride 3-D, stop to admire Optimus Prime standing atop the Nest. How tall does Optimus Prime stand on this building?

a.	11 feet	c.	132 feet
b.	28 feet	d.	280 feet

47. ★★★ As you enter the Nest you will find an ancient hieroglyphics tablet with the Transformers language imprinted on it. What is this language called?
    a. Cybertronian   c. Klingon
    b. Sindarin   d. Na'Vi

48. ★ When entering the Nest, according to the authorized personnel warning sign, an unauthorized presence is what kind of breach?
    a. Protocol   c. government procedure
    b. facilities   d. Security

49. ★★ As you enter the facility you will be greeted by Sonya Bradley, what is her official title?
    a. Security enforcement   c. Hero recruitment officer
    b. Alien/Human relations   d. Human engineering

50. ★★ As you hear the general speaking, what does the S in NEST stand for?
    a. Superior   c. Space
    b. Subordinate   d. Species

Did you know?
The NEST facility has many buttons and switches surrounding you. Feel free to play with these, they are designed to keep you busy during your time in the queue.

The Great Universal Studios Orlando Scavenger Hunt

51. ★★★ As you look around at the controls, find the chart of Transformers silhouettes. Name the transformer in the top row, second from the left.
    a. Optimus Prime
    b. Bumblebee
    c. Sidewinder
    d. Rampage

52. ★★★ Continue your scan of the Transformer silhouettes. What is the name of the image on the bottom row, third from the left?
    a. Rampage
    b. Ravage
    c. Ratchet
    d. Frenzy

53. ★ As you listen to the history of the Transformers, how was their home planet of Cybertron destroyed?
    a. Meteor hit
    b. Collision with another planet
    c. War
    d. Metal mining

54. ★★ Continue watching the monitors throughout the queue. What do the Decepticons seek on Earth?
    a. Uranium
    b. The AllSpark
    c. Sam Witwicky
    d. Mikaela Banes

55. ★★ What item does the transformer call you out for having in your possession?
    a. Ice cream
    b. Cotton candy
    c. A pretzel
    d. A churro

56. ★ As Megatron intercepts the signal, what name does he call you with his last warning?
    a. Weeds
    b. Infidels
    c. Insects
    d. Slaves

57. ★★ As you enter your vehicle and start your journey, which Decepticon traps you in his vortex while you try to evade Megatron?

	a.	Devastator		c.	Ravage
	b.	Overkill		d.	Scavenger

58. ★ When Evac asks, "What do we do?", what is Megatron's response?
    - a. Run while you can
    - b. Give the Allspark to me
    - c. Beg for mercy
    - d. Time to die

59. ★ Which transformer saves you when you are falling off the building?
    - a. Optimus Prime
    - b. Bumblebee
    - c. Ratchet
    - d. Bonecrusher

60. ★ What name does Optimus call you by when he congratulates you on your mission?
    - a. Autobots
    - b. Decepticon destroyers
    - c. Human alliance
    - d. Freedom fighters

61. ★★ What color is the car you see to your left as you finish your mission?
    - a. Red
    - b. Blue
    - c. Green
    - d. Yellow

Did you know?

As you come to the end of your ride, you will see Megatron above you. Watch closely as the eyes glowing red begin to fade and go dark. Megatron is finally dead as you come to the unload area.

New York Street

Become a real New Yorker for a day as you wander through the streets of New York. Stop off at classic New York landmarks like 30 Rock or The New York Public Library.

When you are ready for a rest, stop in for a cold one at O'Rourke's for a pint or indulge in your favorite Italian food. Take in a monster movie come to life on The Revenge of the Mummy but beware of this cursed theater. Be sure to get your tickets for The Tonight Show starring Jimmy Fallon and race through New York before you leave.

Did you know?

As you enter the New York section of Universal Studios Florida, look up at the windows of the Metropolis Tribune building. The name Charlie Gundaker appears in the window. This is a tribute to the senior vice president of attraction development for Universal Studios.

Race Through New York Starring Jimmy Fallon

1. ★★★ Which famous actor left his blue shirt behind as you look through the window in front of Jimmy Fallon Race Through New York?
   - a. Tom Hanks
   - b. Bill Paxton
   - c. Robert Redford
   - d. Jimmy Fallon

> ### Did you know?
> As you enter the hall for Jimmy Fallon Race Through New York, you will see many of the incarnations of the NBC logo throughout the history of the network.

2. ★★ As you look in the windows of the building, find the newspapers hanging from hooks. What is the name of the newspapers you see?
   - a. The Metropolis Times
   - b. The Times Tribune
   - c. The Metropolis Tribune
   - d. The New York Tribune

3. ★★ As you look through the front windows at the newspaper offices, what soda pop advertisement is pinned to the cork board?
   - a. Twister Pop
   - b. Citrus Twister
   - c. Cola Twister
   - d. Twister Cola

> ### Did you know?
> The advertisement for Twister Cola is a nod to the attraction previously housed within this building, Twister – Ride It Out. This attraction starred Bill Paxton and let the audience experience a cyclone first hand.

The Great Universal Studios Orlando Scavenger Hunt

4. ☆ As you wander through the exhibits in the lobby, find the monochromatic camera. In what year was this camera retired from service?
   a. 1947
   b. 1954
   c. 1955
   d. 1996

5. ☆ Find the case for *The Tonight Show* host Steve Allen, what is the title of the sheet music sitting on the piano?
   a. *This could be the start of something*
   b. *Unforgettable*
   c. *This could be the end of something*
   d. *The Flintstones* theme

Bonus Question:

6. ☆☆☆ As you look at the display for Johnny Carson, what was the name of the character he played that wore the hat in the display?
   a. Carnac
   b. Carmine
   c. Carson
   d. Carnac

7. ☆ Which of *The Tonight Show* hosts only hosted this show for one year?
   a. Conan O'Brien
   b. Jay Leno
   c. Jack Paar
   d. Steve Allen

8. ☆☆ What child's toy do you see sitting on the floor of the Jimmy Fallon display?
   a. Telephone
   b. Xylophone
   c. Bugle
   d. Lawn mower

Did you know?

As you head up the stairs and are waiting for your ride, find the shamrock emblem on the stage. This is an exact replica of the mark for Jimmy Fallon at 30 Rock.

9. ★★ As Jimmy Fallon took the stage for the first time to host *The Tonight Show*, how many years had passed since it was filmed in New York?
   a. 4   c. 30
   b. 20   d. 40

10. ★ As you get your racing goggles and they begin the pre-show, what does the flashing sign above the stage read?
    a. Applause   c. Buckle up
    b. Quiet   d. Hang on

11. ★★ As Jimmy gives you a list of the New York landmarks you are about to see, which of these is *not* on his list?
    a. Empire State Building   c. Time Square
    b. Statue of Liberty   d. Central Park

Bonus Question:

12. ★★★ When you arrive back out on New York Street, walk to the New York public library façade at the end of the street. Find the words "Beauty, Old yet ever new, Eternal voice, and inward word". What famous poem are these words from?
    a. "The Shadow and The Light"   c. "A Red Red Rose"
    b. "How Soon Hath Time"   d. "Sonnet 18"

13. ★★ As you read the façade of the library building, which of these is not one of the dedications of the Lenox Library?
    a. Fine Arts   c. History
    b. Literature   d. Music

The Great Universal Studios Orlando Scavenger Hunt

14. ★★ To the right of the New York Public Library façade, you will find a consulate of what republic?
    a. French
    b. Polish
    c. Hungarian
    d. Czechoslovakian

15. ★ Find the I. Stein building on New York street. What does this store sell?
    a. Fine Furs
    b. Fine Clothing
    c. Fine Jewelry
    d. Fine Wine

Bonus question:

16. ★★★ Across the street from Macy's stands The Priscilla Hotel. What famous film features this hotel?
    a. *Mary Poppins*
    b. *Thoroughly Modern Millie*
    c. *Victor Victoria*
    d. *The Princess Diaries*

17. ★★ Find the black antique car parked at the curb. What year does this car represent?
    a. 1939
    b. 1964
    c. 1929
    d. 1901

The Revenge of the Mummy

18. ★ What is the name of the theater hosting The Revenge of the Mummy attraction?
    a. Bijou
    b. Imperial
    c. Pantages
    d. Paradise

19. ★★ As you enter the hot set, find the sign for the extras. What are they required to leave behind?
    a. Modern items
    b. Food and drink
    c. Friends
    d. Scripts

> ### Did you know?
> As you walk through the queue of the Revenge of the Mummy attraction you will come into a room with a warning on a large chest. Do you dare place your hand in the lid? Dare and see what happens.

20. ★★ As you enter your ride vehicle and begin your journey, what does the mummy promise you if you follow him?
    a. Eternal life
    b. Riches
    c. Revenge
    d. Rule over the earth

> ### Did you know?
> There is a very small King Kong statue in the treasure room as a nod to the attraction that occupied this building before The Revenge of the Mummy.

21. ★ As your ride vehicle stops at a dead end, what creatures come out to greet you?
    a. Snakes
    b. Scorpions
    c. Mummies
    d. Scarab beetles

22. ★ As you see Brendan Fraser at the end of your ride, he says he would have enjoyed his interview more if he had what?
    a. Gotten paid
    b. Cup of coffee
    c. Been warned about the curse
    d. Treated like a star

23. ★★ As you exit your ride take a moment to look at the notices within the glass case. Where was the missing cast member last seen?

    a. Changing film
    b. Setting up the scene
    c. Getting latte
    d. Massaging Brendan Fraser

> ### Did you know?
> As you walk along the New York area of Universal Studios Florida, you will come across O'Rourke's Bar and Grill. Notice the proprietors name on the sign, this is a reference to the film *The Godfather*. Kelly O'Rourke is one of the characters from this iconic film.

24. ★ As you walk along the streets of New York find the Blue Brothers stage. Across the street you will see a sign for a flat to let, what child's toy sits on the fire escape next to this sign?
    a. Hula Hoop
    b. Wagon
    c. Roller skates
    d. Pogo stick

25. ★★ Just below you will find a market. Look in the window and you will see three cans of mustard on the shelf. What brand is on the label?
    a. Coleman's
    b. Heinz
    c. Iona
    d. Elite

26. ★★ How much is a can of pork and beans according to the sign?
    a. 25¢
    b. 51¢
    c. 35¢
    d. 15¢

Bonus Question:

27. ★★★ You will come across Embryo Books on Delancey street, what famous film is this a reference too?
    a. *Breakfast at Tiffany's*
    b. *My Fair Lady*
    c. *Roman Holiday*
    d. *Funny Face*

28. ★★★ The logo for Embryo Books is an open book, what famous poem is written on this book?
    a. The Road Not Taken
    b. The Lady of Shalott
    c. A Red Red Rose
    d. The Raven

> **Did you know?**
> As the end of this street you will find the neon sign for the Kitty Kat Club. This fictional business is a nod to the famous Kit Kat Club from the film classic *Cabaret*.

29. ★★ Find the alley next to Hackenburg's appliance store. Across the alley is a music store. Find the neon sign and finish the words, "Piano _____."
    a. Rolls
    b. Keys
    c. Music
    d. Tuning

30. ★★ Down the alley, you will find the barber shop. How much is a children's haircut?
    a. $2.50
    b. $2.00
    c. $5.00
    d. $20.00

31. ★★★ Look closely and you will find the name of the barber, what is his name?
    a. Tom
    b. Bob
    c. Max
    d. Jack

32. ★★★ Continue your exploration of the alley and find the bronze plaque for the London Assurance. What year was this established?
    a. 1270
    b. 1970
    c. 1920
    d. 1720

33. ★ Leroy Piper has a business in this area. He sells second hand what?

	a.	Clothing	c.	Roses
	b.	Furniture	d.	Jewelry

34. ★★ Back on the main street you will find the sign for Miss Alma's Ballroom dancing. How many beautiful girls are there to dance with?
    a. 25
    b. 45
    c. 35
    d. 3

35. ★ Head back to New York street and find the arcade. What horror film poster hangs in the shadow box on the right side of the entrance?
    a. *The Black Cat*
    b. *Frankenstein*
    c. *Curse of the Mummy*
    d. *The Creature from the Black Lagoon*

36. ★★ Across the street from the arcade you will find a Pawn broker shop. As you read the awning, which of these is *not* one of the items they specialize in?
    a. Luggage
    b. Jewelry
    c. Watches
    d. Gold

37. ★★ As you read the sign post on the corner, what arcade is down this alleyway?
    a. Long Island
    b. Coney Island
    c. Cayman Island
    d. Staten Island

38. ★★★ Look into the window of the Manhattan Motor Repair. What brand of sewing machine do you see in the window?
    a. Viking
    b. Toyota
    c. Singer
    d. Brother

39. ★★★ What famous person adorns the cover of Time magazine framed on the wall of Manhattan Motor Repair?
    a. Douglas MacArthur
    b. Governor Earl Long
    c. President Roosevelt
    d. Clark Gable

40. ★ Along this street you will find a fire zone sign, what does this sign prohibit?
    a. No standing
    b. No parking
    c. No dog walking
    d. No outdoor fires

41. ★★ As you come to the end of New York street you will find the Union City News. As you stand before this shop, what sort of photos do they sell?
    a. Passport
    b. Family
    c. Professional
    d. Landscape

42. ★★★ Find the stack of National Geographic's in the window. According to the cover story, what are known as Spain's "Fortunate Islands"?
    a. The Hawaiian Islands
    b. Easter Island
    c. Galapagos Islands
    d. Canary Islands

43. ★★★ Find the issues of People Magazine on the racks to your left, what famous actress adorns the cover of the first magazine published on July 28, 1954?
    a. Ava Gardner
    b. Janis Paige
    c. Janis Joplin
    d. Elizabeth Taylor

Did you know?

Next door to Ben and Jerry's ice cream you will find a red brick building with a bronze plaque that reads, "Hudson Street Home for Girls. Robert L. Ward Headmaster." This plaque is a nod to the film *Annie* in which Little Orphan Annie is housed in this girl's home before being adopted by Daddy Warbucks.

44. ★★ Find Rosie's Irish Shop. In the window find the plaque with the Irish saying. "May your blessings outnumber the _____."
    a. Four leaf clovers   c. Shamrocks
    b. Leprechauns   d. Isles

45. ★ Stand on the corner and find Danny Flannery Music. Which of these is *not* one of the instruments listed on the window?
    a. Coronet   c. Drums
    b. Clarinet d. Cello

46. ★★ To the left of Danny Flannery Music, find the window marked with the name WM. F. O'Brien, what does this company sell?
    a. Art supplies   c. Dinosaur DNA
    b. Anti-shark cages   d. Military Miniatures

47. ★ At Michael's Bar and Grill, stop for a moment at the front of this shop. What type of game is advertised on the window?
    a. Snooker   c. Pool
    b. Billiards d. Bumper pool

48. ★★ What brand of billiard chalk do you find within the pool hall?
    a. Master   c. Silver Cup
    b. Hathaway d. Kiss Shot

49. ★★ What is the subject of the photograph beneath the telephone in the pool hall?
    a. Football c. Billiards
    b. Baseball d. Boxing

San Francisco

It's time to spend the day in the fog drenched city of San Francisco as you stroll along the waters edge and stop in for a bite to eat. Take in the sight and sounds of this city by the bay for a time on your adventures through Universal Studios Florida.

Race through the streets with your favorite street racers as the Fast and the Furious lets you become one of Dom's gang.

1. ★ As you stand at the corner of South St. and Water St. you will find a Walgreen Drugs. How much are the zipper bags you see advertised on the window?
   a. $1.79
   b. .79¢
   c. .37¢
   d. .20¢

2. ★★★ In the window of Walgreen Drugs, you will find several ceramic bottles. Find the label for Chondrus Crispus, what is this more commonly known as?
   a. Spanish moss
   b. Ice Cream
   c. Irish moss
   d. Baking soda

3. ★★★ On the wall you will find a license for the pharmacy. Whose name is printed on this certificate?
   a. Alfred Klein
   b. Robert Klein
   c. Alfred Newman
   d. Thomas Gates

4. ★ Find the advertisement for the health elixir. Which of these is not one of the cures on the list?
   a. Voting democrat
   b. Delusions of grandeur
   c. Tasteless humor
   d. Hiccups

5. ★ Just below the health elixir sign, what sort of cigarettes does Walgreen Drugs sell?
   a. Menthol
   b. Sweet breath
   c. Asthma
   d. Low calorie

6. ★ What product does Aunt Angela's sell in Walgreen Drugs?
   a. Catnip
   b. Butter cookies
   c. Flower seeds
   d. Scalp conditioner

7. ★ On your travels stop near the water. What is the fine for fishing off the dock according to the posted sign?
   a. $10.00
   b. $1,000.00
   c. $10,000.00
   d. $100.00

8. ★ Find the large bronze statue in the square, what prominent figure does this statue salute?
   a. Carl Laemmle
   b. Lew Wasserman
   c. Ronald Meyer
   d. Charles O. Baumann

9. ★ Find the old fashion ice cream shop sign on your way down the street. How many flavors do they sell?
   a. 17
   b. 31
   c. 12
   d. 170

Catherine F. Olen

Richter's Burger Co.

10. ★★ As you walk through Richter's Burger Co., find the advertisement for the world's safest baby carriage. What is the correct price on this earthquake proof carriage?
    a. $25.60
    b. $24.60
    c. $26.40
    d. $25.40

11. ★★ Above you in the main room you will find a drum set. Which of these is the correct name of the band on the bass drum?
    a. Sherman and the Shakers
    b. Tommy and the Tremors
    c. Billy and the Breakers
    d. Alex and the Aftershocks

Did you know?

Notice the paint cans that have spilled from above on the advertisement for Spillman Paint Supply. Richter's is full of little tongue in cheek nods to the earthquake of 1906.

Fast & Furious: Supercharged

12. ★★ As you enter the queue for Fast & Furious: Supercharged, find a sign advising you not to talk to which person on staff?
    a. Machine operator
    b. Foreman
    c. Crane operator
    d. Mechanic

> ### Did you know?
> As you walk through the garage, stop for a moment to look at the large black tool chests around the room. Each has the name of one of the crew. If you look closely at the blue tool chest, you will find a sticker that state, This Car runs on Beetle Juice. This is a nod to the Beetle Juice Graveyard Revue show that occupied this area of Universal Studios Florida.

13. ★★ As you walk through the garage, admire the racing cars throughout. In the second room, find the sign "support your local mechanics." Finish this line, "We can't fix your _____, but we can fix your ride."
    a. Driving
    b. Problems
    c. Life
    d. Relationship

14. ★★★ Nearby, find a bulletin board with many notices pinned to it. In the upper left corner there is a menu from which restaurant?
    a. Dom's
    b. Walkers
    c. Letties
    d. Tarantino's

15. ★★ In the lower right corner of the bulletin board, find the handwritten note. According to the top of the note, "Look! It's from _____!"
    a. Lettie
    b. Marie
    c. Mia
    d. Susan

16. ★★★ Through the chain link, you will see a wall with several license plates. Resting on the toolbox with the bowling pin, which of these is the correct California license plate you see?
    a. BK2TFTR
    b. DSASTR
    c. OUTATIME
    d. 2FST2FRS

> ### Did you know?
> As you walk through the garage, you will find the vehicle Tej calls his Mona Lisa created for The Fast and the Furious Supercharged.

17. ★★ Before you leave the garage area, you will find another bulletin board near the locker area. What hotel is featured on the guest guide and map of San Francisco?
    a. Hotel Californian
    b. Hotel Majestic
    c. Fairmont San Francisco
    d. St. Francis

> ### Did you know?
> You will notice several advertisements for the San Francisco area. This is in keeping with the area of the park where the Fast & Furious attraction is housed.

18. ★★★ As you enter the pre-show area with the lockers and kitchen area, find the after-party advertisement. Where is this party being held?
    a. San Francisco Garage
    b. Disaster Garage
    c. Beetlejuice Garage
    d. Sullivan's Garage

> ### Did you know?
> Notice the small notes on the bulletin board and refrigerator, you will see the group harassing Agent Hobbs on these notes.

The Great Universal Studios Orlando Scavenger Hunt

> ### Did you know?
> The Fast & Furious attraction pays respect to actor Paul Walker in this room. You will find a mechanics shirt with the name Brian, Walkers character, as well as pictures of Walker and tennis shoes beneath the locker waiting for Brian to return.

19. ★★ When you enter the control room, look at the map drawn on the board. According to mission Strongarm, what is the "go time"?
    a. 6:30
    b. 4:45
    c. 6:45
    d. 6:55

20. ★ Find the Protect Your Eyes notice on the wall as you walk through the building. Which department posted this notice?
    a. Security
    b. Carpentry
    c. Engineering
    d. Mechanics

21. ★★ Find the wanted poster for Owen Shaw. In what year was the picture of Shaw taken?
    a. 2012
    b. 2009
    c. 2006
    d. 2007

22. ★★★ As you look at the list of Shaw's associates, where was Stella Badillo born?
    a. Sweetwater, TN
    b. El Paso, TX
    c. Unknown
    d. Savannah, GA

23. ★ Find the sign posted by the San Francisco Board of Health. What activity is unlawful according to this sign?
    a. Street racing
    b. Spitting
    c. Loitering
    d. Littering

> ### Did you know
> Just before you get to the load area, find three electrical boxes on the wall. Notice the initials and numbers on each box. EQ-061990 refers to Earthquake which opened in June 1990, DI – 012008 for Disaster January 2008 and FF -032018 for Fast & Furious March 2018. If you look closely, notice each of the boxes is time worn with the opening of each attraction in this spot.

24. ★★ As you enter the loading area, find a clip board with a yellow post in note hanging on the wall. Which member of the Fast & Furious team wrote this note?
    a. Tej
    b. Pat
    c. Dom
    d. Brian

> ### Did you know?
> If you walk through the single rider queue you will find Dominic Toretto's trophy case with keys and pink slips from the cars he has won. Read the titles closely and you will find the DeLorean owned by Doctor Emmett Brown in *Back to the Future*, the Ford own by the Weasley family in Harry Potter and the Bandit from the classic film *Smokey and the Bandit*.

> ### Did you know?
> Down near the water is a full-size replica of the shark from *Jaws*. Don't miss an opportunity to pose with this menacing figure from this classic film.

The Great Universal Studios Orlando Scavenger Hunt

25. ★★ As you look across the water, find the billboard for Upton & Sons Sport Fishing. Which of these is the phone number for Upton & Sons?
    a. 555-8297
    b. 555-9782
    c. 363-8000
    d. 864-8377

26. ★★ Continue down the street and find several store fronts along the sidewalk. As you stand before the record store look in the window at the albums on display. What is the name of the album by the Quint Trio?
    a. *My Favorite Part of the Movie*
    b. *One Hit Wonders*
    c. *Katy's In Charge*
    d. *Here's to Swimming' With Bow Legged Women*

The Wizarding World of Harry Potter™ - Diagon Alley™

As you enter the magical mystical world of Harry Potter, you will explore the well-known shops and attractions that bring you right to the heart of the Harry Potter books. Become a wizard yourself when you don your robes, hold your wand in hand and transport yourself to a world where anything is possible.

Make a deposit at Gringotts™ or grab a bite at the Leaky Cauldron before racing through the vaults below the famous Gringotts bank.

Be very careful, or you make take a wrong turn and wind up in the dark and mystic Knockturn Alley™.

Knight Bus

1. ★★★ As you approach the Knight Bus, stop for a moment to chat with the shrunken head next to the driver's seat. What is the name of this shrunken head?
    a. Dre Head
    b. Dr. Dre
    c. Dread Head
    d. Jack

> **Did you know?**
>
> Spend some time with the Knight Bus driver and his companion. They will interact with you and take pictures in front of The Knight Bus.

2. ★★★What color beads will you find in the hair of the shrunken head on the Knight Bus?
    a. Red and Blue
    b. Blue and Green
    c. Green and Yellow
    d. Yellow and Red

Hogwarts™ Express – King's Cross Station

3. ★★ Before you enter Kings Cross Station, stop to read the arrival and departure schedule. Which platform does the train leaving for Newcastle use?
    a. 9
    b. 3
    c. 13
    d. 19

4. ★★ The train departing to Doncaster leaves at which time?
    a. 10:49
    b. 10:47
    c. 12:43
    d. 12:49

5. ★★ The 10:43 train from York has what status in the comments?
    a. Late
    b. Boarding
    c. Cancelled
    d. On time

6. ★★What do you read on the comments for the arrival from Watton-At-Stone?
    a. Cancelled
    b. On time
    c. Late arrival
    d. Missing

7. ★★As you walk through the station, find the sign for left luggage and lost property. Which of these is *not* one of the items you see on the sign?
    a. A key
    b. A stroller
    c. A handprint
    d. An umbrella

> ### Did you know?
> As you walk through Kings Cross Station and find the wall for platform 9 ¾, look for a luggage cart. If you watch carefully, you can see your loved ones disappear through the wall to the secret platform.

> ### Did you know?
> As you come through the wall and arrive at platform 9 ¾, look around at the luggage waiting on the platform. You will see Harry Potters beloved owl waiting for you in his cage. Watch as his head turns to greet the waiting passengers.

8. ★ As you excitedly wait for your ride on the Hogwarts Express, what is the number on this train?
    a. 5972
    b. 5279
    c. 7952
    d. 2579

9. ★★★ As you take your seat and begin your journey, you will see an owl flying next to your train. What do you see flying in the distance?
    a. More owls
    b. Dementors
    c. Ron and Harry
    d. Hagrid

10. ★★ As you listen in on the conversation between Ron and Hermione, what is Ron looking for?
    a. A compartment
    b. Scabbers his rat
    c. The food trolley
    d. A safe place to hide

11. ★★★ As you cross through to the wizarding world, you will see a flock of birds in the sky. What shape do the birds create momentarily in the sky?
    a. An owl
    b. A wand
    c. A broomstick
    d. A skull

12. ★ What do you hear someone scream out in the corridor of the train?
    a. Death eaters!
    b. Dementor!
    c. Lord Voldemort!
    d. Spiders!

13. ★★ What item does Ron ask for from the Trolley after they defeat the dementor?
    a. Pumpkin pasties
    b. Bertie Bots
    c. Chocolate frog
    d. Licorice spider

14. ★ What character from Harry Potter is at the station to greet you when you arrive in Hogsmeade?
    a. Hagrid
    b. Professor Dumbledore
    c. Professor Snape
    d. Harry Potter

15. ★★ As you travel back from Hogsmeade to Kings Cross Station, you will see Ron, Hermione and Harry in the hall looking for what?
    a. Hagrid
    b. The food trolley
    c. An empty compartment
    d. Ron's wand

16. ★★★ What mythical creature do you see flying next to the train while you travel?
    a. A Hippogriff
    b. A Phoenix
    c. A Unicorn
    d. A Thestral

17. ★★★ What is the name of the mythical creatures you see running alongside the train through the forest?
    a. Satyrs
    b. Centaurs
    c. Pegasus
    d. Werewolves

18. ★ How do the Weasley twins advertise their store Weasleys' Wizard Wheezes as you go along your journey?
    a. A large banner
    b. Skywriting
    c. Yelling at you
    d. Fireworks display

19. ★★ What flavor are the spiders you see in the corridor?
    a. Chocolate
    b. Pumpkin
    c. Licorice
    d. Strawberry

20. ★★ As you travel through London, which enchanted form of transportation do you encounter?
    a. The Knight Bus
    b. Ron's flying car
    c. Nimbus 2000 broomstick
    d. Hagrid's flying motorbike

21. ★★★ Which character from Harry Potter greets you with a wave as you arrive at Kings Cross Station?
    a. Lucius Malfoy
    b. Sirius Black
    c. Mad Eye Moody
    d. Tom Riddle

Did you know?

As you walk along the apartments that hide Diagon Alley, look carefully at the windows. You will see the familiar figure of Kreacher the house elf peering down at you from time to time.

> **Did you know?**
>
> Hidden in the shadows is the entrance to Diagon Alley. Walk through the bricks and leave the real world behind as you enter the enchanted world of Diagon Alley. Listen carefully as you will hear the sound of the bricks rubbing against each other to make the opening for you to walk through.

Quality Quidditch™ Supplies

22. ★ As you look in the window of Quality Quidditch Supplies, which broomstick is displayed for you to admire?
    a. Nimbus 2000
    b. Firebolt
    c. Oakshaft 79
    d. Comet 140

23. ★★ As you step into this store you will see several cans stacked up on the top of the shelves. What sort of broom care do these cans provide?
    a. Sandpaper
    b. Bristle cleaner
    c. Wood oil
    d. Wax

24. ★ Which quidditch team do you see posing for you in the enchanted poster?
    a. Falmouth Falcons
    b. Puddlemere United
    c. Appleby Arrows
    d. Chudley Cannons

Weasleys' Wizard Wheezes

25. ★★ As you enter Weasleys' Wizard Wheezes, Find the notice for this week's managers specials. What will you receive for a little less than you expected when you buy a Decoy Detonator?

	a.	Nose-biting Teacup	c.	Self-writing Quill
	b.	Screaming Yo-Yo	d.	Hex Off

26. ★★ As you enter Weasley's, look up at the figure riding the tightrope above your head. Which Harry Potter character do you see on the tightrope?
    a. Dolores Umbridge   c. Bellatrix Lestrange
    b. Rita Skeeter   d. Peter Pettigrew

27. ★ Find the stairs in the center of the store. Read the words written on the stairs and finish this line, "More magical _____ up this way."
    a. Wonders   c. Mayhem
    b. Tricks   d. Madness

Did you know?

Look high above you to the ceiling of Weasleys' Wizard Wheezes and enjoy the fireworks display on the enchanted surface.

Did you know?

If you look in the window of Weasleys' watch the display for Puking Pastilles. The poor display keeps filling the bucket continuously throughout the day.

28. ★ As you watch the large animated man trapped in the building of Weasleys' Wizard Wheezes tip his hat to you, what do you see when he raises the hat?
    a. Rabbit   c. Owl
    b. Cat   d. Rat

The Great Universal Studios Orlando Scavenger Hunt

29. ★ If you circle the building to the back of Weasley's, read some of the advertisements painted on the back wall. What sort of animal is the backdrop for Dung Bombs?
    a. Donkey
    b. Whale
    c. Lion
    d. Elephant

30. ★ Just above Sugarplum's Sweet Shop, you will find a sign for the store selling musical instruments. Which of these is *not* one of the items listed on the sign?
    a. Bagpipes
    b. Sitars
    c. Lutes
    d. Harps

31. ★ As you step into Sugarplum's Sweet Shop, stop for a moment to read the menu on the wall. What sort of jelly item are they offering?
    a. Gerbil
    b. Turtle
    c. Slug
    d. Serpent

32. ★ Sugarplum's offers fudge in the shape of what creature?
    a. Lizards
    b. Mudskippers
    c. Mosquitos
    d. Flies

Did you know?

To the left of Sugarplums, you will find an archway. Look up at the apex of this archway and you will find a statue of Dobby the house elf watching over Diagon Alley.

Did you know?

To the left of Dobby, you will see a large area with owls perched. The decorators of Universal Studios even went so far as to add bird poop to the perches to show the birds have been coming and going for a very long time.

Bonus Question:

33. ★★★ Find the shop for Bowman E. Wright Blacksmith. What famous item from Harry Potter did this blacksmith create?
    a. The golden snitch
    b. The Sorcerer's stone
    c. The horcruxes
    d. The Marauder's map

34. ★★★ Continue reading the advertisements on the buildings. How many years is Fire Whiskey aged?
    a. 29 years
    b. 38 years
    c. 39 years
    d. 42 years

35. ★★ The advertisement for Madame Glassy's shoe polish says to apply with just a swift what?
    a. Kick
    b. Swish
    c. Flick
    d. Brush

36. ★ In the center of this area you will find a statue of a mermaid. What creature do you see crawling up the side of the bowl in front of the mermaid?
    a. Rat
    b. Lizard
    c. Frog
    d. Snail

37. ★★ At the corner, you will find a placement agency for what type of creature?
    a. Retired ogres
    b. Witches and Warlocks
    c. Hornless unicorns
    d. House elves

38. ★ Next to Gregorovitch's fine wands, look at the wall with the advertisement for a newspaper. On what day of the week can you have your innermost conundrums unraveled?
    a. Wednesday
    b. Friday
    c. Monday
    d. Tuesday

The Great Universal Studios Orlando Scavenger Hunt

39. ★ Find the Museum of Muggle Curiosity's. What muggle item adorns the sign for this museum?
    a. A television
    b. A computer
    c. A bathtub
    d. A telephone

40. ★★ In the window of the Museum of Muggle Curiosity's find the microwave oven. Which of these options is *not* one found on the reheat menu?
    a. Curry
    b. Hamburger
    c. Chinese
    d. Pasta

41. ★★ Which of these is the third choice on the defrost options for the microwave oven?
    a. Bread
    b. Meat items
    c. Meat joints
    d. Beef bones

42. ★★★ Find the Hoover vacuum cleaner. Just above the brand you will find the words, "By appointment" to whom?
    a. King George V
    b. J. Edgar Hoover
    c. James Murray Spangler
    d. William H. Hoover

43. ★ As you look around at the business signs, what product does Archibald Bennett sell?
    a. Sports equipment
    b. Baby strollers
    c. Wigs
    d. Christmas ornaments

Gringotts™ Money Exchange

> **Did you know?**
> Speak to the teller inside Gringotts™ Money Exchange. He will interact with you and answer questions for guests.

Catherine F. Olen

The Leaky Cauldron

> **Did you know?**
> As you approach The Leaky Cauldron, stop for a moment and watch the sign. The cauldron you see on this sign actually leaks.

44. ★★ Before you order your meal at the Leaky Cauldron, be sure to read about the specialties. Which of these is *not* on the menu?
    a. Toad in the hole
    b. Mutton tongue stew
    c. Guinness stew
    d. Scotch eggs

45. ★★★ As you wait for your turn to order your meal, take a look at yesterday's specials. What delicacy is paired with the fried partridge eggs?
    a. Newt sausage
    b. Crispy bat wings
    c. Newt tails
    d. Slug soup

46. ★★ Before you leave The Leaky Cauldron, you will find a small sign advising patrons to leave quietly after what hour?
    a. Midnight
    b. Daybreak
    c. The wizarding hour
    d. The witching hour

47. ★ Within the Leaky Cauldron you will find the wanted poster for Sirius Black. The poster advises you to avoid using what against this man?
    a. Force
    b. Wands
    c. Magic
    d. Reason

The Great Universal Studios Orlando Scavenger Hunt

48. ☆ Across from the Leaky Cauldron you will find a shop that sells what jellied delicacy?
    a. Eels
    b. Cranberries
    c. Beef
    d. Tongue

49. ☆ Find the eel pie in the window. How many eel heads do you see poking out of the crust?
    a. 9
    b. 6
    c. 10
    d. 7

50. ☆ As you stand before Potage's Cauldron shop you will see a large stack of cauldrons to the left of the store. How many cauldrons do you see?
    a. 12
    b. 21
    c. 14
    d. 17

Flourish and Blotts Booksellers

51. ☆☆ In what year was Flourish and Blotts booksellers established?
    a. 1454
    b. 1545
    c. 1954
    d. 1554

52. ☆☆☆ As you stand before Flourish and Blotts, read the signs for this shop. Which of these is *not* one of the items they advertise for sale?
    a. Spells
    b. Potions
    c. Charms
    d. Herbology

53. ☆☆ In the window, you will find a monster book in his cage, what do you see at the bottom on the cage?
    a. Newspapers
    b. Bones
    c. Shredded paper
    d. Wood chips

54. ★★ In the window of Flourish and Blotts you will find a large stack of books on their side. Finish this title, "The Decline of _____ Magic."
    a. Black
    b. Pagan
    c. Muggle
    d. Traditional

55. ★★ As you continue reading the titles in this stack of books, finish this title, "Omens, Oracles and the _____."
    a. Dark arts
    b. Sacrifice
    c. Origins of magic
    d. Goat

56. ★ Next door to Flourish and Blotts you will find the offices for The Daily Prophet. Finish the tag line on the sign for this newspaper, "The wizarding worlds beguiling _____ of choice."
    a. Newspaper
    b. Broadsheet
    c. Tabloid
    d. Source

Did you know?
Use the knocker on the door of the Daily Prophet and listen above as you hear voices coming from inside.

Did you know?
Next door to The Daily Prophet you will find Spindlewarps, in the window you will find the same self-knitting needles Mrs. Weasley uses.

Madam Malkin's Robes for All Occasions

57. ★★ As you stand in front of Madam Malkin's Robes for All Occasions look up at the second story window. What famous piece of clothing do you see from the Harry Potter films?
    a. Ron's formal robes
    b. Hermione's ball gown
    c. Harry's school robes
    d. Dumbledore's robes

> **Did you know?**
> Stand before the full-length mirror at the back of the shop. You will hear the mirror give her opinion of you. Sometimes the words are not favorable, you have been warned.

> **Did you know?**
> Be sure to admire the white gown on display at the back of the shop. The enchanted skirt changes as you watch.

Mr. Mulpeppers Apothecary

58. ★★★ Find the display of plants in Mulpepper's Apothecary. In what year was Mulpepper's established?
    a. 1611
    b. 1106
    c. 1161
    d. 1206

59. ★★ In the window display for Mulpepper's Apothecary you will find a chalkboard advertising what bat part?
    a. Wings
    b. Claws
    c. Spleen
    d. Brain

60. ★★ As you walk down Diagon Alley, read some of the signs above you. How many years has Brew and Stews been in business?
    a. 100
    b. 200
    c. 300
    d. 400

61. ★ Magical Cures and Preventions offers classes to combat fear of what?
    a. Death eaters
    b. Lord Voldemort
    c. Flying
    d. Dementors

Florean Fortescue's Ice Cream Parlor

62. ★ As you stand before Florean Fortescue's Ice Cream Parlor, look up at the advertising on the wall above. What sort of treat is advertised?
    a. Ambrosia
    b. Pudding
    c. Ice Milk
    d. Tapioca

63. ★ Read the sign for today's suggestion at Florean Fortescue's Ice Cream Parlor. Finish the name of this flavor "Earl grey and _____."
    a. Whiskey
    b. Lemon
    c. Ale
    d. Lavender

Harry Potter and the Escape from Gringotts™

Did you know?

Before you enter Gringotts to open your account, stop and admire the magnificent dragon atop the building. She will breathe fire at you every so often if the weather permits.

The Great Universal Studios Orlando Scavenger Hunt

64. ★ As you wind through the outdoor queue, read the advertisements for Gringotts. Which type of vaults are *not* available?
    a. Enchanted
    b. Magic proof
    c. Safety
    d. Dragon guarded

65. ★ The Gringotts banner inside the doorway advertises the safest place for several items. Which of these is *not* one of the items listed on the banner?
    a. Gold
    b. Jewels
    c. Money
    d. Magical Items

> **Did you know?**
> As you walk through the bank to the goblin at the end, stop for a moment and he will talk to you about opening an account at Gringotts.

66. ★★ As you walk through the halls of Gringotts, notice the newspaper sitting atop one of the tables. Harry Potter is sought for questioning for what reason according to the headline?
    a. The escape of Sirius Black
    b. The death of Albus Dumbledore
    c. The capture of Bellatrix Lestrange
    d. The death of Severus Snape

67. ★★★ At the top of the Daily Prophet you can win a trip to what city?
    a. Shangri-La
    b. Atlantis
    c. Transylvania
    d. Utopia

Catherine F. Olen

> ### Did you know?
> Watch the glass in the doors as you pass through the hallways of Gringotts and you may see some familiar characters behind these closed doors.

68. ★★ What does the goblin find when he opens Bill Weasley's desk drawer looking for vault keys?
    a. Weasleys' Wildfire Whiz-bangs
    b. Love potion
    c. Puking Pastilles
    d. White rat whiskey

69. ★★ What item does Bill pick up and start playing with as you are directed on where to go next?
    a. Spectacles
    b. Spyglass
    c. Pen and paper
    d. Magnifying glass

> ### Did you know?
> As you enter the elevator to take you down to the vault transport, notice the floor moves beneath your feet and the walls move past the elevator car. While this looks and feels like you are really in an elevator, you are not actually moving. You exit on the same level you entered.

70. ★★ As you enter your vehicle and start on your way, which Harry Potter villain stops your car?
    a. Dolores Umbridge
    b. Bellatrix Lestrange
    c. Professor Quirrell
    d. Lucius Malfoy

71. ★★★ What item was Harry Potter going to the vaults to retrieve when you see him?
    a. Money
    b. Horcrux
    c. Dragon
    d. Ring

72. ★★★ What spell does Bill Weasley cast when the dragon appears?
    a. Alohomora
    b. Wingardium Leviosa
    c. Expecto Patronum
    d. Aguamenti

73. ★★ What word does Bellatrix use to describe you when she and Lord Voldemort stop you during your journey?
    a. Traitor
    b. Half-blood
    c. Muggle born
    d. Death eater

> **Did you know?**
> To the left of Gringotts you will find a staircase that leads to nowhere. This area is a forced perspective to create the illusion that Diagon Alley continues further up the hill.

74. ★★ As you look up the stairs to the left of Gringotts, notice a sign for T & T. Which of these is not one of the items they advertise on their storefront?
    a. Dragonskin Jacket
    b. Silk pajamas
    c. Fancy hats
    d. Formals

Ollivanders™

> **Did you know?**
> As you enter Ollivanders, take a look at the area just inside the window. You will see a broom sweeping all by itself.

75. ★ Ollivanders has been making wands since what year?
    a. 382 BC
    b. 382 AD
    c. 832 BC
    d. 832 AD

76. ★★ As you enter Ollivanders, notice the sign above the brooms. "Feel Free to _____ our brooms."
    a. Handle
    b. Sweep
    c. Test-fly
    d. Play quidditch

77. ★★ As the wand fitter explains about the core of each wand, which of these is *not* included in his list of cores?
    a. Dragon heartstring
    b. Phoenix tailfeather
    c. Hippogriff tailfeather
    d. Unicorn hair

78. ★ As you watch the wand fitting, how is the wizard fitted for their wand?
    a. The wand chooses the wizard
    b. By length
    c. The wizard chooses the wand
    d. Go to the gift shop

79. ★★★ What advice does the wand fitter tell you about storing your wand?
    a. Never give it to a friend
    b. Never leave it unattended
    c. Never cast an enchantment on it
    d. Never leave it in your back pocket

---

80. ★★ Next to Ollivanders you will find Weeoanwhisker's Barber Shop. In the window, find the small bottle of shave cream with the man's head on top. What brand do you see on this bottle?
    a. Clean Close Shave
    b. Shave N Save
    c. Wizard Shave
    d. Burma Shave

The Great Universal Studios Orlando Scavenger Hunt

Magical Menagerie

81. ★ Flanking the front door of Magical Menagerie, you will see two magical animals. What muggle animal do they resemble?
    a. Giraffe
    b. Hippopotamus
    c. Zebra
    d. Ostrich

82. ★ Look in the window of Magical Menagerie, what over-sized animal do you see on the perch?
    a. Monkey
    b. Cat
    c. Snail
    d. Flea

> **Did you know?**
> If you walk around the side of Magical Menagerie, you will find a snake in the window. Listen carefully and you will hear him speak to you in Parseltongue.

Bonus question:

83. ★★★ Enter the store and look around at the wonders throughout the store. In the upper corner of Magical Menagerie, you will find a purple magical animal with one horn. This Crumple Horned Snorkack is the favorite creature of which Harry Potter character?
    a. Neville Longbottom
    b. Nearly Headless Nick
    c. Argus Filch
    d. Luna Lovegood

84. ★★★ Find the small red bottles high above you in Magical Menagerie. Which of these is the correct label on these bottles?
    a. Super-Fast Cat Tonic
    b. Superlative Rat Tonic
    c. Super Duper Satyr Grow
    d. Superlative Snake Venom

> ### Did you know?
> High above, you will find an orange cat creature looking down. This animal is known as a Kneazle. Hermione Grangers cat Crookshanks is known to be half Kneazle and was purchased by Hermione from this very store.

85. ★★ The Kneazle that is sitting high above you within Magical Menagerie lays on a box of what sort of creature?
    a. Dancing Doxy
    b. Bouncing Boxy
    c. Flouncing Floxy
    d. Trouncing Troxy

86. ★★ Continue down the street to the left of Gringotts and read some of the signs around you. What does Mrs. Skowers sell?
    a. Clouds
    b. Magical mess remover
    c. Beard bags
    d. Taxi service

87. ★★ In the area to the left of Gringotts, find the blue sign for the society for the reformation of what sort of creatures?
    a. Hags
    b. Death eaters
    c. Warlocks
    d. Trolls

88. ★★ Find the advertisement for Fergus Fungal Budge. What does this product combat?
    a. Athlete's foot
    b. Jungle rot
    c. Stealthy sludge
    d. Ringworm

> **Did you know?**
>
> Notice the black umbrella just above the conveniences. With a wave of your wand this umbrella will not protect you from the rain but rain upon you.

89. ★★ At the end of the road you will find the store Potions for All Afflictions. As you peruse the display of Skelegrow in the window, how many drops are in each bottle?
    a. 110
    b. 11000
    c. 1100
    d. 11

90. ★ What color hat does the man drinking the Skelegrow wear?
    a. Red
    b. Green
    c. Black
    d. White

91. ★★★ High above, you will find many windows with many potions within. Find small jars within the window, the label on mixture 74 reads what?
    a. Scarab beetle
    b. Sloth toe
    c. Horned slugs
    d. Poison frog

92. ★★★ What does the bottle with mixture 34 contain?
    a. Scarab Beetle
    b. Snake bone
    c. Dragon blood
    d. Unicorn tears

Knockturn Alley

> **Did you know?**
>
> Knockturn Alley is known to be the dark side of the wizarding world. Watch yourself as you may come across some unsavory characters as you turn down this part of Diagon Alley.

93. ★★ Find the sign for Fledermaus and Tanner. Finish this part of the signage, "_____ & skin."
    a. Spiders
    b. Wolves
    c. Vultures
    d. Bats

94. ★★ Find the shop for Arachnids Available. Which one of the following is *not* on the sign for this shop?
    a. Web weavers
    b. Good for pets
    c. Bird-eating
    d. Venomous

95. ★★★ Look around in the darkness to find the sign for what sort of lessons for your tarantula?
    a. Domestic spiders
    b. Guard spiders
    c. Un-tame
    d. Speaking

> **Did you know?**
> You will find the windows for the shop selling arachnids covered with newspaper. Watch as the spiders within the shop crawl across the papers.

96. ★★ Find the sign for E.L.M. Undertakers and Embalmers, "Cross over in _____ style."
    a. Spellbinding
    b. Grand
    c. Mesmerizing
    d. Grand

97. ★★ Continue reading the sign for E.L.M. Undertakers and Embalmers. What sort of magical creature is on duty day and night?
    a. Wizard
    b. Witch
    c. Ogre
    d. Fairy

98. ★★★ The Locksmith sign in Knockturn Alley reads that they repair what sort of locks?
    a. Magical
    b. Sinister
    c. Enchanted
    d. Confounded

The Great Universal Studios Orlando Scavenger Hunt

99. ⭐⭐ As you explore Knockturn Alley you will find a set of stairs leading to what sort of shop?
    a. Pawn broker
    b. Sinister toys
    c. Dark arts
    d. Cloaks

> **Did you know?**
> Find the Tattoo parlor within Knockturn Alley and peek through the window to see the artwork come to life. These enchanted tattoos are waiting for their new companions.

> **Did you know?**
> In the center of Knockturn Alley, you will find witches' and wizards waving their wand across the large window containing various skeletons. Be amazed as the large skeleton comes to life and dances for your enjoyment.

Borgin and Burkes™

100. ⭐⭐ Within the sinister shop of Borgin and Burkes find the cursed hand encased in glass. How many muggle owners have perished according to the warning sign?
    a. Fourteen
    b. Nineteen
    c. Ninety
    d. Seventeen

101. ⭐⭐ As you explore the curiosities of Borgin and Burkes, you will find a large object holding umbrellas and canes. What sort of object do you see?
    a. Dragon foot
    b. Wooden leg
    c. Troll foot
    d. Ogre head

> ### Did you know?
> Step to the back of Borgin and Burkes to find one of the vanishing cabinets you have read about. Listen closely and you may hear the chirp of a bird coming from within.

> ### Did you know?
> As you examine the oddities on the shelves of Borgin and Burkes, stop for a moment to inspect the china doll with the broken face. If you look very closely at the broken part of the head and the arm, you will notice human bone concealed beneath.

102. ★★ Across from Borgin and Burkes, you will find a sign advertising what sort of repellant?
    a. Mandrake eating snails
    b. Human eating spiders
    c. Snake eating fish
    d. Flesh-eating slug

103. ★★ Find the sign for the chimney sweeps within Knockturn Alley. What mythical creature do you find within the chimney on this sign?
    a. Witch
    b. Death Eater
    c. House elf
    d. Dementor

Did you know?

Find the window with the shrunken heads staring out at you. Wave your interactive wand and these heads will serenade you as they sing. If you stay to listen to most of their songs, you will hear *Show me the way to go home*. It may sound familiar to those of you who have seen the classic Universal Studios film, *Jaws*. In the scene where main characters are on the boat drinking together, they sing this very song. This stands as another nod to the Jaws attraction that was retired to create Diagon Alley.

World Expo

Join the Men in Black™ as they save the Earth from alien attacks. Join them for your on the job training and see if you can join their ranks.

If you can complete your training by outshooting your fellow trainees and earn your status as one of the top Men in Black.

Men in Black™: Alien Attack

1. ✯✯ As you enter the building for Men in Black Alien Attack and begin wandering the halls, stop for a moment at the index of rooms within the building. What is the name on the conference room?
    a. Roswell
    b. Saturn
    c. UFO
    d. Covert

2. ✯✯ Continue reading the index of rooms. What area of the building will you find referenced on the fifth line from the top?
    a. Fingerprint removal
    b. Oxygen free zone
    c. Alien resources
    d. Human resources

The Great Universal Studios Orlando Scavenger Hunt

3. ★★ As you walk past the breakroom, what brand of coffee do you find on the counter?
   a. Keurig
   b. Maxwell House
   c. Yuban
   d. Folgers

4. ★★★ Stop for a moment to read the notices in the glass board just past the break room. On the blue sheet for auditions for *Oklahoma,* which creatures are auditioning at 2730 hours?
   a. Bipeds who move well
   b. Bipeds who sing
   c. Multipeds who sing and move well
   d. Multipeds who can't sing or dance

5. ★★★ Find the memo offering a 20% discount on vacation packages to the galactic kingdom of the six moons. Where is this resort located?
   a. Rigel 7
   b. Paradiso IV
   c. Earth
   d. Saturn's 5th moon

6. ★★★ Continue scanning the bulletin board across from the break room until you find the Men in Black criminal report. On this report you will find the description of the tattoo under distinguishing marks. What does the tattoo say?
   a. Aliens make better coffee
   b. Aliens rule, humans drool
   c. Uranus or bust
   d. Mom

Did you know?

On the criminal report narrative, you will notice the officer describes a van full of people and the alien did not respond to questions asked in Spanish. This is a description of the opening scene of the very first *Men in Black* film.

7. ★★★ On the MIB cafeteria menu, notice some of the dishes offered have an * after them. What does this star mean?
   a. May contain alien parts
   b. May not taste like actual food
   c. Vegan dish
   d. Not for human consumption

8. ★★ As you enter the main room for Men in Black headquarters, notice a newspaper sitting atop one of the desks. According to the headline, what sort of creature ate the news reporter?
   a. Lizard
   b. Sloth
   c. Dinosaur
   d. Cockroach

9. ★★★ As you read the newspaper story about the UFO shot down by Russia, in what year was the photograph taken?
   a. 1977
   b. 1987
   c. 1997
   d. 2007

Did you know?

As you step into your vehicle and begin your training, hit the aliens swinging from the lampposts for as long as you can.

Once the aliens in the windows appear, begin hitting them for as long as you are able. Your gun will allow you to shoot aliens multiple times.

Aim for the exhaust port on the rival car and you will send your opponents into a spin. This will make it impossible for them to shoot or gather points.

When the big bug appears Hold your red button down as this will allow you to add huge bonus points to your score.

Springfield: Home of the Simpsons

Hang out with your friends the Simpson's when you step into Springfield. Explore the games of Krustyland or stop in the Kwik-E-Mart for an ice cold Squishee. Get a picture with Bart, Lisa, Homer and Marge or dare to meet Sideshow Bob. Wind up your day with an ice-cold drink at Moe's Tavern as you immerse yourself in the world of the Simpson's.

1. ★ As you enter Springfield, stop to admire the Springfield billboard. According to the sign, what is Springfield the home of?
    a. The nuclear power plant
    b. The Isotopes
    c. Duff brewery
    d. The Simpsons

2. ★ Find Android's Dungeon, the comic book store. What reason does the sign give for the store being closed?
    a. At Lard Lad Donuts
    b. Buying new comic books
    c. On a date with Agnes
    d. Bi monthly Sci-Fi Con

3. ★★ Chief Wiggum has crashed his police car, he's holding a donut, how many sprinkles do you see on his donut?
   a. 12
   b. 9
   c. 5
   d. 27

4. ★ What does the police cars vanity license plate read?
   a. #1POLICE
   b. RALPHDAD
   c. #1DOOFUS
   d. SPRNGFLD

> ### Did you know?
> Hang out with police Chief Wiggum for a quick picture and watch the lights and siren of his car alert you to danger periodically.

5. ★★ As you stand in front of the Duff Brewery you will find the seven Duffs. Which of these is not one of the seven Duffs?
   a. Queasy
   b. Edgy
   c. Drunky
   d. Remorseful

> ### Did you know?
> Stand before the statue of Springfield founder Jebediah Springfield. In the Simpsons series, the statue depicts the founder after he killed a bear with his own hands. Later, Lisa Simpson finds out this was in fact a lie but the statue remains as the town keeps the secret.

Fast Food Blvd

6. ★★ As you enter the Fast Food Blvd, which of these is *not* one of the food options you see?

	a.	Cletus Chicken Shack	c.	Lisa's Teahouse of Horror
	b.	The Frying Dutchman	d.	Dead Lobster

7. ★★ Find the large mural of Springfield on the wall, what animals do you see Moe chasing?
    a. Dolphins
    b. Pandas
    c. Killer Whales
    d. Dogs

8. ★★ Find Marge and Lisa standing in front of the Aztec theater. What movie is shown on the marquee?
    a. Face Smasher 6
    b. McBain
    c. The Itchy and Scratchy Movie
    d. The Contrabulous Fabtraption of Professor Horatio Hufnagel

9. ★★ Find sideshow Mel pushing a baby carriage. Which Simpsons character do you see in the carriage?
    a. Santa's Little Helper
    b. Mr. Teeny
    c. Laddie
    d. Snowball II

10. ★★★ Which Simpson's character is changing the tire on the school bus for Springfield Elementary School?
    a. Groundskeeper Willie
    b. Otto Mann
    c. Principle Skinner
    d. Miss Hoover

11. ★★ Which Simpsons character is being bullied by Jimbo Jones, Kearney and Dolph in the mural?
    a. Martin
    b. Ralph
    c. Milhouse
    d. Wendell

12. ★★ As you continue your exploration of the restaurant, find the mural of the Simpsons characters. Which character is represented by number 123?
    a. Bubbles
    b. Sea Captain
    c. Wendell
    d. Fallout Boy

13. ★★ As you continue your examination of the characters, which character is represented in number 316?
    a. Dr. Julius Hibbert
    b. Bleeding Gums Murphy
    c. Sideshow Bob
    d. Krusty the Clown

14. ★★★ Which number represents Chief Wiggum's wife Sarah?
    a. 245
    b. 254
    c. 279
    d. 369

15. ★★★ What number does Krusty the Clown's father have on this chart?
    a. 804
    b. 1048
    c. 408
    d. 72

Moe's Tavern

16. ★ Stop off at the love tester as you walk into Moe's Tavern. What does the highest level read on the love tester?
    a. Casanova
    b. Hot Tamale
    c. Cold Fish
    d. Luke Warm

17. ★ Find the sign for Old Time Fancy Pants Whiskey. What number is on the label?
    a. No. 5
    b. No. 50
    c. No. 7
    d. No. 8

18. ★ What product does Snake have his picture on?
    a. Mugger Moonshine
    b. Burglar Booze
    c. Criminal Rotgut
    d. Jailbird Gin

19. ★ What year is shown on the label for Grandpa's Spirits?
    a. 1986
    b. 1886
    c. 1889
    d. 1989

The Great Universal Studios Orlando Scavenger Hunt

> **Did you know?**
> Don't miss an opportunity to pose with Barney for a picture while he looks into his empty beer glass.

20. ★★ Find the picture of Homer, Principle Skinner, Barney and Apu singing. What was the name on their musical group?
    a. Party Posse
    b. The Second-Best Band in America
    c. Hooray for Everything
    d. The B Sharps

21. ★ As you look around Moe's Tavern, what does Moe claim this is the birthplace of?
    a. The Flaming Homer
    b. Bill Clinton
    c. The Flaming Moe
    d. Bleeding Gums O'Sullivan

22. ★★ Find the picture of Homers softball team. What number appears on Barneys jersey?
    a. 13
    b. 5
    c. 26
    d. 7

23. ★ Find the neon sign for the Flaming Moe. What feeling is just a Flaming Moe away?
    a. Drunkenness
    b. Giddiness
    c. Happiness
    d. Delirium

---

24. ★ As you leave Moe's Tavern, find the front of Cletus Chicken Shack. What do the sacks stacked out front contain?
    a. Claws and Wings
    b. Day Old Beaks
    c. Chicken Feathers
    d. Chicken Thumbs

Catherine F. Olen

> ### Did you know?
> Cletus Chicken Shack sells Chicken Thumbs. Don't miss an opportunity to try this Cletus delicacy.

> ### Did you know?
> As you stand on the porch of Cletus Chicken Shack, listen for the chickens clucking in the nearby crate.

> ### Did you know?
> Across the street, you will find a full size Duffman in front of the Duff Brewery. Don't miss an opportunity to get your picture taken with this Springfield celebrity.

The Kwik-E-Mart

25. ★ Before you enter The Kwik E Mart, stop for a moment to read the advertisements in the window. Buzz Cola is the choice of what generation?
    - a. Crappy
    - b. High
    - c. New
    - d. Cheap

Bonus Question:

26. ★★★ What celebrity took over for Apu in season five of the Simpsons to research a movie role to play a convenience store clerk?
    - a. Steve Carrell
    - b. Alec Baldwin
    - c. James Woods
    - d. Luke Perry

27. ★ Find the bags of Nature's Own Cat Litter. What is this product made with?
    a. Beach sand
    b. Wood chips
    c. Reused cat litter
    d. Quick sand

28. ★ Continue looking round the Kwik E Mart. Finish the label "Much Ado About _____."
    a. Muffins
    b. Stuffing
    c. Nuttin'
    d. Something

29. ★ On the package of Dry Diapers, how much is the capacity of each diaper?
    a. 5 ounces
    b. 5 cups
    c. 5 pounds
    d. 5 liters

Bonus Question

30. ★★★ What is the name of the baby that is featured on the package for Dry Diapers?
    a. Baby Gerald
    b. Baby Maggie
    c. Baby Anoop
    d. Baby Kearney

> **Did you know?**
>
> You will see boxes of Frosted Krusty-O's on the shelves around the shop. In one episode of *The Simpsons*, Bart went to the hospital after eating a jagged metal Krusty-O that was a prize in the cereal box.

31. ★ Which beloved Simpsons character sits on the bench outside the Kwik E Mart drinking a soda?
    a. Bart
    b. Lisa
    c. Maggie
    d. Milhouse

32. ★ What flavor Squishee is being advertised on the window of the Kwik E Mart?

a.	Chutney	c.	Bacon Lime
b.	Anchovy Peach	d.	Jalapeno Raspberry

33. ★★ How much does it cost for a local call in Springfield at the pay phone?
    a. .25¢
    b. $2.00
    c. .50¢
    d. $1.00

> **Did you know?**
>
> Lift the receiver on the Springfield payphone and listen to the voice on the other end. Which Simpsons character do you hear?

34. ★ What name does Nelson call you when he says the phone is for you?
    a. Dip wad
    b. Dummy
    c. Dingus
    d. Dilly

35. ★ Take a look at the fence behind the Kwik-E-Mart to see Chief Wiggum holding a wanted poster. Who is he looking for?
    a. El Barto
    b. Fallout Boy
    c. Jimbo Jones
    d. Homer Simpson

Kang and Kodos' Twirl 'N' Hurl

36. ★★ Read the billboard for the Twirl 'N' Hurl. When do they want you to tell people how fun this ride is?
    a. Right after you go on it
    b. Before you go on it
    c. When you enter the theme park
    d. Never, keep it a secret

37. ★ How many little aliens do you need to be as tall as to ride the Kang and Kodos' Twirl 'N' Hurl?

| a. 4 | c. 1 |
| b. ½ | d. 40 |

The Simpson's Ride

> **Did you know?**
> Before you walk through the open mouth of Krusty the Clown, stop and look directly above you. Krusty's uvula is dangling down from the roof of his mouth.

38. ★★ Find the park map for Krustyland and fill in the blank for Number 15, "Captain Dinosaurs Pirate _____."
    a. All singing and dancing revue
    b. Merchandise advertisement
    c. Rip-off
    d. Robotic ride

39. ★★ In Krusty's Haunted Condo, there are 999 what?
    a. Fake ghosts
    b. Robotic zombies
    c. Sheets dressed up like ghosts
    d. Unhappy teen employees

40. ★★ On the map you will find Moe's Tunnel of _____?
    a. The next best thing to love
    b. Shame and rejection
    c. Groping in the dark
    d. Spooky stuff in the dark

41. ★★ The last item on the list is number 40, get _____ by Kang and Kodos?
    a. Probed
    b. Abducted
    c. Slimed
    d. Taken away

42. ★★ Read some of the posters for the attractions you will find at Krustyland. Which Simpson's character is fea-

tured as the mummy on the poster for Screamatorium of Dr. Frightmarestein?
   a. Barney
   b. Cletus
   c. Milhouse
   d. Side Show Bob

43. ★★ Which of Bart and Lisa's friends are featured on the poster for Radioactive Man the Ride?
   a. Bart and Milhouse
   b. iHiltoHiltohhNelson and Kearney
   c. Sherri and Terri
   d. Martin and Ralph

44. ★★★ What Simpsons character is featured on the Krusty's Wet and Smoky Stunt Show poster?
   a. Troy McClure
   b. Radioactive man
   c. Sideshow Mel
   d. McBain

45. ★★★ Which is these ladies of Springfield is *not* found on the poster for the Isotop-ettes?
   a. Lurleen Lumpkin
   b. Patty Bouvier
   c. Paris Texan
   d. Edna Krabappel

46. ★ What sort of simulator can you find in Krustyland as you read the posters?
   a. Amusement park
   b. Yard work
   c. Presidential election
   d. Larry Totter Wizard

47. ★ Find the movie poster starring Maggie Simpson as you work your way through the queue. What is the name of this horror film?
   a. The Longest Daycare
   b. The Day the Pacifiers Died
   c. Prisoner of the Playpen
   d. A Baby for all Seasons

48. ★★ As you enter the pre-ride area, look around at the different booths. Which Simpson's character mans the information booth?

a. Abe Simpson   c. Old Jewish Man
b. Jasper   d. Hans Moleman

49. ★★ Read some of the brochures that sit atop the counter of the information booth. What do you get for free with a drink at Moe's Tavern?
    a. Panda   c. Expired pickled egg
    b. Date with Barney d. A date with Moe

50. ★★ Find the brochures and finish the title for "A Hot Time in the Old _____."
    a. Broken down drive-in   c. Tire yard
    b. Small town   d. Church basement

51. ★ Which attraction is slated for demolition according to the information sign?
    a. The Yard Work Simulator   c. Radioactive Man; The Ride
    b. The Traumanator Coaster   d. Poochies Toddler Kennel

52. ★ What is the name of the crew member for the ride that you see hanging on the wall in the pre-boarding area?
    a. Side show Robert   c. Side show Barney
    b. Side show Krusty   d. Side show Homer

53. ★ As you read the list of items at the snack bar, which of these is not one of the candies available?
    a. Cotton candy   c. Stringy candy
    b. Linen candy   d. Flannel candy

54. ★ What is the fried item on the menu at the snack bar?
    a. Fried sushi   c. Fried plantain's
    b. Fried chewing gum   d. Fried sugar

55. ★ Near the snack bar you will find the Hi Striker game. What is the top level you reach if you ring the bell?

a.	Krusty	c.	Schlub
b.	Superheroes	d.	Normal hero

56. ★★ On the Itchy and Scratchy wheel of pain, which word is paired with eyeballs?
    a. Twist   c. Pop
    b. Gouge   d. Switch

> **Did you know?**
> The Simpson's Ride uses the same building as the predecessor, The Back to the Future Ride. The engineers used the exact same ride movements, animating the action on the screen to match the previous ride movements.

57. ★★ What body part is paired with pinched on the Itchy and Scratchy Wheel of Pain?
    a. Earlobe   c. Uvula
    b. Bellybutton d. Eyeball

58. ★★ Look for the tarot cards surrounding Madam Manjulas the Future Looker-atter. Which Simpson's character is seen on the card for death?
    a. Death   c. Flanders devil
    b. Mr. Burns   d. Bart Simpson

59. ★★ As your pre-show video begins, you see Krusty the Clown. How much longer does he say you will be in line?
    a. 45 hours   c. 45 minutes
    b. 45 days   d. 4.5 hours

60. ★★ As you take your seat and your ride begins, which Simpson's character says, "You're all gonna die."?
    a. Nelson   c. Krusty
    b. Sideshow Bob d. Homer

61. ★★ As you ride through the dinosaurs that begin to crash, what does Homer say he hates?
    a. Theme parks
    b. Dinosaurs
    c. Chain reactions
    d. Animated who's-it-what's

62. ★ What marine animal does Bart ride trying to save you from the water show?
    a. Dolphin
    b. Giant squid
    c. Sea lion
    d. Killer whale

63. ★ Which Simpson's character saves you from Sideshow Bob?
    a. Snake
    b. Sideshow Mel
    c. Krusty
    d. Maggie

64. ★★ What does Sideshow Bob offer Maggie Simpson if she destroys Springfield?
    a. A giant bottle
    b. Her pacifier
    c. A nap
    d. To be his minion

65. ★★ Why does Marge tell Maggie to get the tourists out of her mouth?
    a. They're dirty
    b. No snacking between meals
    c. You don't know where they've been
    d. You might choke

66. ★★ Which Simpsons' characters surprise the Simpsons after they think they are home?
    a. Kang and Kodos
    b. Fang and Kiddos
    c. Sideshow Bob and Maggie
    d. Kirk and Luanne

67. ★ After you exit the Simpson's Ride, walk around the midway games. At the Dunk and Flunk, which character is seen with a dunce cap on his head?
    a. Ralph Wiggum
    b. Bart Simpson
    c. Nelson Muntz
    d. Martin

68. ★ At the Whack a Rat game, read the epitaphs on the headstones. What were Itchy's last words?
    a. Scratchy was my friend
    b. Another mouse bites the dust
    c. Aaaagh, this hurts!
    d. First Jerry, now me

69. ★★ At the Strike 3 game, what is the name of the character seen on the sign?
    a. Cocoa Bean
    b. Lard Lad
    c. Capital City Goofball
    d. Smiling Joe Fission

Woody Woodpecker's KidZone

Go back to the age of classic cartoons as you explore the Woody Woodpecker KidZone. Visit with Woody Woodpecker and his niece and nephew as you race along. Spend some time with everyone's favorite purple dinosaur Barney or get soaked with Curious George as you step into the pages of a storybook.

Play with Fievel and his friends as you shrink down to the size of a mouse and top off your time with a ride on a flying bike at the E.T. Adventure.

SpongeBob StorePants

1. ★ Before you enter SpongeBob StorePants, look in the window at the advertisements. What kind of prices does Mr. Krabs advertise?
   a. Soggy bottom
   b. Deep Fried
   c. Sky high
   d. Salt water

2. ★ Find the blue surfboard with the yellow stripe down the middle in the window. How many payments of $9.95 will you make on this surfboard?
   a. 10
   b. 7 ½
   c. 3,000
   d. 100

3. ★ As you enter SpongeBob StorePants, read the subsidiary sign. Find the little sign for the lost animal. Which animal are they looking for?
   a. Snail
   b. Sea cucumber
   c. Jellyfish
   d. Starfish

4. ★★ Find the Krab policy sign near the registers. What is the punishment for shoplifters?
   a. Drowning
   b. Forced to work here
   c. Walk the plank
   d. Babysit Mr. Krabs

5. ★★ What percentage restocking fee does Mr. Krabs charge customers for return merchandise?
   a. 100%
   b. 30%
   c. 10%
   d. 300%

6. ★ As you wander through Bikini Bottom, read some of the sign around the store. What does this store give free with each purchase?
   a. Bad attitude
   b. Receipt
   c. Bag
   d. Jellyfish

E.T. Adventure

7. ★★★ In what year did audiences experience *E.T. the Extra-Terrestrial* in theaters?
   a. 1992
   b. 2002
   c. 1982
   d. 2008

8. ★★★ Which famous director introduces the E.T. Adventure?
   a. Steven Spielberg
   b. James Cameron
   c. John Houston
   d. Ridley Scott

9. ★★ What is the name of E.T.'s teacher?
   a. Alienus
   b. Elliot
   c. Bottanicus
   d. Germanus

10. ★★ How far away is E.T.'s home planet from Earth?
    a. Three million miles
    b. Three billion light years
    c. three billion miles
    d. Three million light years

11. ★★ What item do you need to make the journey with E.T. back to his home planet?
    a. A spaceship
    b. Interplanetary passport
    c. Money
    d. Space suit

Did you know?

You will give your name to one of the cast members inside the building and you will be given your interplanetary passport. Once you give this card to the cast member at the load area, E.T. will know your name and thank you personally at the end of your ride.

Did you know?

As you hop on your bike and ride through the forest, watch the basket mounted on the front of your bike. You will see E.T. pop up from time to time.

> ### Did you know?
> As you fly over Los Angeles, look at the full moon and you will see E.T. fly across with Elliot and his friends.

> ### Did you know?
> Before your time at the E.T. Adventure is through, visit the E.T. closet and get your picture with E.T. in the costume Gertie dressed him in.

Fievel's Playland

12. ★★ As you enter Fievel's Playland, stop for a moment to read the newspaper, what date was this paper released?
    a. July 4, 1982
    b. July 4, 1892
    c. July 4, 1882
    d. July 4, 1893

13. ★★★ If you read the newspaper article about traveling across the great unknown, how long does the trip take by train?
    a. 30 days
    b. 3 months
    c. 3 years
    d. 3 days

14. ★ Find the stroller parking sign, what common object are the words written on?
    a. A button
    b. A quarter
    c. A penny
    d. A dime

15. ★ Which gang is shown on the wanted poster you can pose with for pictures?
    a. Cat. R. Waul gang
    b. Butterfly gang
    c. Halve knifes gang
    d. Stillwell gang

The Great Universal Studios Orlando Scavenger Hunt

16. ★ Find several spools of thread near the benches. Which of these is not one of the colors of thread you see?
    a. Red
    b. Blue
    c. Green
    d. Yellow

17. ★★ As you explore Fievel's Playland, you will notice the bench made from a ruler What city was the ruler manufactured?
    a. Hollywood, California
    b. Tombstone, Arizona
    c. Dowling, Ohio
    d. Orlando, Florida

18. ★ Find the large red book that rests with a pair of glasses nearby. What is the title of this book?
    a. *The Life and Times of Wiley Burp*
    b. *The Life and Times of Fievel Mousekowitz*
    c. *The Life and Times of Tiger the Cat*
    d. *The Life and Times of Cat. R Waul*

19. ★★ Along your exploration of Fievel's Playland, you will find a slide. What object is used to create this slide?
    a. Spatula
    b. Harmonika box
    c. Pencil box
    d. Measuring tape

20. ★ In which year was Professor Largman's Hoof Linament established according to the carton you find?
    a. 1977
    b. 1877
    c. 1788
    d. 1881

21. ★★ Along the jungle gym, you will find several playing cards standing on end. What animal is shown on the Jack?
    a. Dog
    b. Cat
    c. Mouse
    d. Horse

22. ★ Find the box of Arachnid Sox, how many pair are in this box?
    a. 10
    b. 6
    c. 8
    d. 12

23. ★ Near the Sautéed Sardine can, you will find a notice, "No Fishing, No _____."
    a. Wading
    b. Hunting
    c. Playing
    d. Swimming

Woody Woodpecker's Nuthouse Coaster

24. ★★ As you work your way through the queue for Woody Woodpecker's Nuthouse Coaster, try to figure out some of the signs you see. Which of these is the correct words for the sign with the kitchen pot?
    a. Are you a potty mouth?
    b. Are you a pot roast?
    c. Are you a pot pie?
    d. Are you a crack pot?

25. ★★ Find the sign for the board of directors. Who is the product tester?
    a. You
    b. Woody
    c. Splinter
    d. Knothead

26. ★ Find the box of practical jokes. Which character wrote return to sender on this crate?
    a. Knothead
    b. Splinter
    c. Woody
    d. Winnie

> ### Did you know?
> As you get closer to the loading area, read the words left on the red fence. Notice these words were made by the woodpecker's beaks drilling small holes in the fence.

27. ★ As you wait at the load area for your ride, find the green saw hanging across from you. How many eyes do you see on this saw?
    a. 6
    b. 11
    c. 12
    d. 5

Curious George Goes to Town

28. ★ What sort of animal is Curious George?
    a. Bear
    b. Dog
    c. Monkey
    d. Cat

> **Did you know?**
>
> As you enter the Curious George goes to Town area, notice the yellow prints on the ground. Curious George has left his footprints as he explores this area of the park.

29. ★ According to the storybooks, George is happy because he is visiting the man with what color hat?
    a. Yellow
    b. Brown
    c. Blue
    d. Green

30. ★ Find the picture of Cecily the giraffe, what does the sign beneath her read?
    a. World's happiest
    b. World's cutest
    c. World's richest
    d. World's smartest

31. ★ As you explore the red and yellow big top, what does the Animal Show sign say about today's show?
    a. Cancelled
    b. Postponed
    c. Delayed
    d. Starting

32. ★★ Find the hotel, which animal silhouette broke through the sign on this building?
    a. Giraffe
    b. Elephant
    c. Rhino
    d. Monkey

33. ★ Find the hotel phone, what sort of calls will you make by pulling the handle?
    a. Collect calls
    b. Toll calls
    c. Long distance calls
    d. Soggy calls

34. ★ Find the Stay Dry Cleaners in the town. What color is the shirt hanging up to dry outside?
    a. Yellow
    b. Red
    c. Blue
    d. Green

35. ★ Find the newspaper box outside the Morning Star News. What does the headline read on the newspaper?
    a. Monkey joins the circus
    b. Monkey buys a circus
    c. Monkey finds a friend
    d. Monkey sets animals loose

36. ★ What sort of household item is hanging from the pink building next door to the newspaper office?
    a. Sink
    b. Bathtub
    c. Washing machine
    d. Clock

37. ★★ If you walk into the post office, find the wanted poster for Curious George. What is the phone number on this poster?
    a. 555-4321
    b. 555 – 1212
    c. 555 – 1234
    d. 555-4231

38. ★ Which of these is *not* one of the names on the post office boxes you see in the Post Office?
    a. L.E. Phant
    b. Wally Rus
    c. P.G. Lett
    d. G. Raffe

39. ★ As you step into the bakery, what is the price for a donut?
    a. $2.00
    b. .5¢
    c. .25¢
    d. .10¢

40. ★ Stop to look at the tower in the center of the town. Which of these animals is *not* smiling at you from the tower?
    a. Horse
    b. Lion
    c. Seal
    d. Zebra

> ### Did you know?
> Before your time with Curious George is through, be sure to get a picture of this monkey as he rides atop a stream of water in the fountain.

Barney's Backyard

> ### Did you know?
> Barney's Backyard is a safe interactive play space for Barney's littlest friends. Join in the fun as you watch your little people explore the world around them while they grow their curiosity about the world.

> ### Did you know?
> Within Barney's Backyard, you will find several multicolored stepping stones. Step on these shapes and listen to the sounds that come from each.

Hollywood

Step onto the street of Hollywood and experience tinsel town up close and personal. Shop and eat with the stars in this glittering mecca of movies and movie stars.

Do not be surprised if you come across some of the most recognizable Hollywood stars like Marilyn Monroe or Lucille Ball. You may even see some of your favorite animated characters come to life like the gang from Scooby Doo and the Simpsons.

Before your day in Hollywood is through, stop at the Horror Make up show to learn the history of the horror movie industry and see the latest Hollywood make up techniques.

1. ✯✯✯ As you begin your time in the Hollywood area, step on the sidewalk in front of Beverly Hills Boulangerie you will find one of the city signs. At what address does the city of Beverly Hills offer public parking?
    a. 12305 Fifth Helena Dr.
    b. 8221 Sunset Blvd
    c. 440 N. Camden Dr.
    d. 6925 Hollywood Blvd

The Great Universal Studios Orlando Scavenger Hunt

2. ★★ As you walk down the street in the Hollywood area, you will find yourself in front of the world famous Mocambo's. In what year was this night club established?
   a. 1943
   b. 1901
   c. 1993
   d. 1939

3. ★ Find the Ralphs neon sign in Hollywood. What is this storefront selling?
   a. Clothing
   b. Shoes
   c. Groceries
   d. Watches

4. ★★ As you look in the window of Ralphs, what animal shape is the egg holder?
   a. Rooster
   b. Cow
   c. Pig
   d. Nest

5. ★ Continue down the street in Hollywood until you come to Brandstatters Café Montmartre. For $1.25 on the menu the choices are New York Cut Sirloin Steak or what entree?
   a. Vegetable Appetizer
   b. Roast and Vegetables
   c. Grilled Steak
   d. Half Spring Chicken

Universal Orlando's Horror Make-up Show

6. ★ As you stand in front of the theater for The Universal Orlando's Horror Makeup Show, in what theater does this show take place?
   a. Hollywood Theater
   b. Pantages
   c. Dorothy Chandler
   d. Grauman's Chinese Theater

7. ★★ As you enter the building for The Universal Orlando's Horror Makeup Show, take a moment to look over the props. Look in the center glass case and you will

~ 85 ~

find the make-up kit of what famous Universal movie monster actor?
- a. Lon Chaney
- b. Bela Lugosi
- c. Vincent Price
- d. Boris Karloff

8. ★ On the wall you will find a list of the Universal Studios monster films by date. In what year was the film *The Bride of Frankenstein* released?
- a. 1933
- b. 1935
- c. 1954
- d. 1975

9. ★ In what year was the Universal Studios monster film *The Thing* released?
- a. 1982
- b. 1993
- c. 1999
- d. 1923

10. ★★ As you take a look at the photographs from the great monster films. What did the prop master use as spider webs in the classic horror film *Dracula* starring Bela Lugosi?
- a. String
- b. Spider webs
- c. Rubber cement
- d. Boogers

11. ★★ Movie actor and make-up artist Lon Chaney was known as "The Man of 1,000 _____."
- a. Characters
- b. Faces
- c. Monsters
- d. Make-ups

12. ★★★ As you continue your exploration of the lobby area, you will come across a full-size statue of which Universal Studios movie monster?
- a. Dracula
- b. Frankenstein monster
- c. The Mummy
- d. The Phantom of the Opera

13. ★★ As you read the cards on the history of the Universal Studios monster films, which famous actor turned down the role of Frankenstein in 1931?
    a. Lon Chaney
    b. Vincent Price
    c. Bela Lugosi
    d. Boris Karloff

14. ★★ As you read the card for the great director Alfred Hitchcock, what was his nickname in Hollywood?
    a. Master of the movies
    b. Master of horror
    c. Master of Hollywood
    d. Master of suspense

15. ★ What is the name of the killer in the *Childs Play* series of films?
    a. Chucky
    b. Tommy
    c. Billy
    d. Chummy

16. ★ At the corner in front of the Universal Studios Horror Makeup Show, you will find the gates of what movie studio?
    a. Universal Pictures
    b. Esoteric Pictures
    c. Monumental Pictures
    d. Energetic Pictures

Mel's Diner

17. ★ As you approach Mel's Diner, take a look at the antique cars parked outside. What is the make and model of the black car with the tail fins?
    a. Pontiac Chieftan
    b. Buick Roadmaster
    c. Dodge Meadowbrook
    d. Chevy Bel Air

18. ★ Find the bright yellow car with the plexiglass hood. In what year was this Deuce Coupe manufactured?
    a. 1952
    b. 1932
    c. 1982
    d. 1942

Schwab's Drug Store

> ### Did you know?
> A long-standing Hollywood legend states that movie star Lana Turner was discovered at the lunch counter of Schwab's Drug Store by director Mervyn LeRoy. This, along with many other Hollywood legends is completely false.
> Turner was discovered at the age of 17 by William Wilkerson, publisher of the Hollywood reporter at The Top Hat Café. Wilkerson referred Turner to agent Zeppo Marx, brother of the famous Marx Brothers comedians.

19. ★★ As you look around Schwab's Drug Store note the sign listing the different medication they are selling. What is the cost of a cold remedy at Schwab's?
    a. .25¢
    b. .15¢
    c. .59¢
    d. .50¢

20. ★★ Which product advertisement offers the stepping stones to health?
    a. Coca Cola
    b. Morton's salt
    c. Double Mint Gum
    d. Hershey's Syrup

21. ★★★ What photo of a famous movie star do you see on the right wall on Schwab's?
    a. Elizabeth Taylor
    b. Jean Harlow
    c. Jane Mansfield
    d. Lana Turner

22. ★★★ Just below the large Prescription sign you will find a photograph of one of the most famous actors from the

golden age of Hollywood. What is the name of this heart-throb of the silver screen?
   a. Jimmy Stewart
   b. Clark Gable
   c. Rudolph Valentino
   d. Kirk Douglas

23. ★★ Continue your explorations of Schwab's Drugstore and you will come across a bottle with the label that reads, Hostetter's Celebrated Stomach Bitters. What percent alcohol is this product by volume according to the label?
   a. 4%
   b. 10%
   c. 2%
   d. 44%

24. ★★ While looking at the products on the shelves, find the canister with the circus clown adorning the can. What product does this package contain?
   a. Bandages
   b. Candy
   c. Talcum
   d. Aspirin

25. ★ How much is a package of gum if you purchase it from the vending machine inside of Schwab's Drugstore?
   a. .01¢
   b. .10¢
   c. $1.00
   d. .11¢

---

26. ★★★ At the corner of Hollywood Blvd. you will see The Brown Derby Hat Shop. This store is a re-creation of The Brown Derby in Hollywood. What did the original Brown Derby sell?
   a. Hats
   b. Men's clothing
   c. Food
   d. Women's clothing

27. ★ Find the brass plaque commemorating the founder of the Brown Derby. In what year was this restaurant founded?
   a. 1939
   b. 1929
   c. 1829
   d. 1999

Universal's Islands of Adventure

Introduction

Find the adventure of a lifetime at Universal's Islands of Adventure. Explore the far reaches of imagination with your favorite characters from classic films and books.

Step through the pages of your favorite comic books to fly with Spiderman and save the city, Soar high over the theme park on the Hulk or stay one step ahead of Dr. Doom.

Explore mystic islands and step back through time where dinosaurs roamed free. Discover the mythic ape known to live on Skull Island if you have the courage.

Grab your wand, broom and robes and begin your wizard training while enjoying the sights and sounds of your favorite Harry Potter books come to life.

Join the mystical islands of the Lost Continent as you explore the ruins of an ancient temple to find a lost archeologist. Indulge your taste buds at Mythos restaurant voted one of the best theme park restaurants for 2019.

Finally, go back to your childhood with your favorite Dr. Seuss characters and meet the famous Grinch as he comes from Mount Crumit to visit with guests of Seuss Landing.

Port of Entry

Your adventure begins as you step through the gates of Universal's Islands of Adventure and explore the Ports of Entry. Whether you are looking for the latest clothing styles or savor delicious chocolates, you can find them in this charming marketplace. For those looking for Christmas and time of the year, stop by the Christmas shop to find your new favorite Christmas decorations.

Ports of Entry brings just a glimpse of the excitement surrounding you as you begin your day at Universal's Islands of Adventure.

1. ★★ As you enter the gates of Islands of Adventure notice the vehicle parked to your right. What is printed on the life preserver attached to this vehicle?
    a. HMS Turner
    b. HMS Titanic
    c. HMS Pinafore
    d. HMS Lusitania

2. ★★★ As you examine the over packed taxi, what sort of snow equipment do you see?
    a. Snow skis
    b. Snow shoes
    c. Snowmobile
    d. Snow pick

3. ★ Stop for a moment at the camera shop. You will find a mural alongside the entrance. Finish the tag line, "The _____ is mightier than the sword."
   a. Shutter
   b. Photographer
   c. Camera
   d. Lens

> ### Did you know?
> Do not miss the Port of Entry Hoosegow tucked away high above you at the Port of Entry. Notice the broken bars and bed sheets hanging from the window. The prisoners have escaped.

4. ★ Continue your exploration of Port of Entry and find the musical instruments off to your left. Which of these is *not* one of the instruments you see?
   a. Xylophone
   b. Sitar
   c. Bongo
   d. Slit drum

> ### Did you know?
> As you walk through Port of Entry, make sure to get your picture on the tiger, monkey or cheetah and find the rickshaw for some truly unusual photo opportunities.

5. ★ As you walk along the marketplace, find the pillars advertising the wares for sale. What weight are the edible gems sold by?
   a. The karat
   b. The pound
   c. The ounce
   d. The gemstone

6. ★★ Which of these is *not* one of the items you see advertised on the pillars to your right?
   a. Spices
   b. Coffee
   c. Chocolate
   d. Olive oil

7. ★ Find the purple rickshaw parked along the road to your left. What sort of bank is carved on the sign behind the driver seat?
   a. Banana
   b. Blood
   c. Coconut
   d. Pineapple

8. ★★ If you peek inside the rickshaw, what item do you find they are transporting?
   a. Bananas
   b. Coins
   c. People
   d. Fabric

9. ★★★ On the coins you will find a roman numeral, which of these numbers does this roman numeral represent?
   a. 1999
   b. 1196
   c. 1986
   d. 2016

10. ★★ As you read the signs around you, what is the reason that the fire brigade is no longer in the area?
    a. Moved closer to water
    b. Burned down
    c. No fires in the area
    d. Couldn't find any volunteers

11. ★ Find an advertisement for the musician painted on the wall outside one of the shops. What is the name of this master musician?
    a. Professor Hill
    b. Professor Cariatun
    c. Professor Sousa
    d. Professor Caricature

12. ★ Which of these is *not* one of the instruments the professor tutors?
    a. Boom-pah
    b. Magic harp
    c. Concertina
    d. Didgeridoo

13. ★★★ As you come to the Christmas shop, look up at the balcony above. What animals do you see peering down at you?
    a. Parrots
    b. Monkeys
    c. Bears
    d. Cats

> ### Did you know?
> Do not miss an opportunity to stop into the Confisco Grille in Port of Entry. Be sure to look around at the items surrounding you. The Confisco Grille has taken items from the other areas of the park and you will find the items along the walls of this eatery.

Confisco Grill

14. ✯✯✯ Walk through the doors of Confisco Grille and you will notice goods lining the walls. Find Rocky and Bullwinkle, what is the name of the two villains hanging beside them?
    a. Bonnie and Clyde
    b. Boris and Natasha
    c. Boris and Doris
    d. Nero and Cleopatra

15. ✯✯ Find the can of toon paint, what color is in this can?
    a. Primrose pink
    b. Primrose Blue
    c. Primrose Yellow
    d. Primrose Green

16. ✯✯✯ Next to the can of toon paint you will find an artifact with a Writ of Seizure tag on it from The Lost Continent. What is the reason this item was seized?
    a. Confiscated
    b. Impounded
    c. Quarantined
    d. Counterfeit

17. ✯ As you come to the caricature area, read the label on the crates they use for the cashiers. What famous island was box this shipped from?
    a. Hawaiian Island
    b. Philippine Island
    c. Easter Island
    d. Galapagos Islands

18. ★ At the end of Port of Entry, you will find the bakery. What is the correct name for this bakery?
    a. Crescent Moon
    b. Croissant Moon
    c. Cupcake Moon
    d. Crescent Roll Moon

19. ★★ Outside the bakery you will find several crates with ingredients. Which of these is *not* one of the ingredients you see?
    a. Baking powder
    b. Pepper
    c. Flour
    d. Sugar

Marvel Super Hero Island

Step into the pages of your favorite Marvel comic books as you fight crime with your favorite super heroes. Ride through the city with Spiderman, meet Dr. Doom in his secret lair and visit with your favorite super heroes in Marvel Super Hero Island.

Did you know?

As you enter the Marvel Super Hero Island, walk underneath the Hulk roller coaster. Notice the lamp posts? The Project Gamma insignia can be found. This is the project that turned Bruce Banner into the Incredible Hulk.

Did you know?

As you approach the Café 4, look up at the entrance. You will find the Baxter Annex. According to the comic books, this is where the Fantastic Four reside in New York.

The Great Universal Studios Orlando Scavenger Hunt

The Incredible Hulk Coaster

1. ★★ As you approach The Incredible Hulk Coaster, read the warning on the side of the launch tube above you. Whom do you need authorization from to enter the restricted military defense lab?
    a. General Thaddeus Ross
    b. General Stan Lee
    c. General Rick Jones
    d. Jonas Jameson

2. ★★ Enter the queue and find the clearance levels. What level clearance do you need to enter the reactor core control room on level one?
    a. G4
    b. C14
    c. G14
    d. C4

3. ★★ As you read the table for the nano-metabolic conversion chamber unit 3, in what status is the uranium 236?
    a. Stable
    b. In stasis
    c. Active
    d. Unstable

4. ★ As you continue your way through the facility, how many days have they gone without a containment incident according to the sign?
    a. 13
    b. 30
    c. 3
    d. 31

5. ★★ According to the restriction sign in the load area, any personnel showing abnormal behavior or increased what shall be immobilized?
    a. Green color
    b. Hostility
    c. Size
    d. Mobility

---

6. ★★ As you come to the Café 4, what is the name of the fire character you see from *The Fantastic Four*?

a.	The Thing	c.	Human Fireball
b.	Human Torch	d.	Torch Boy

7. ★ As you approach Storm Force Accelatron, how many spinning pods do you see?
    a. 10
    b. 8
    c. 15
    d. 12

8. ★★ Find the Cotton Candy stand on the streets of Marvel Super Hero Island. Which character from the Fantastic Four do you see riding atop this stand?
    a. Metal Surfer
    b. Platinum Surfer
    c. Silver Surfer
    d. Diamond Surfer

> **Did you know?**
>
> Look down at the street as you work your way through Marvel Superhero Island and find the manhole cover. This cover is another nod to the area with Marvel Superhero Island written across the metal surface.

9. ★★ As you continue down the road of Marvel Super Hero Island, stop at the arcade. Which Marvel villain is seen on the sign with the gold game tokens?
    a. Abomination
    b. Venom
    c. Apocalypse
    d. Kingpin

Bonus question

10. ★★★ According to the Marvel universe, which of these is the real name of the villain Kingpin?
    a. Victor Von Doom
    b. Wilson Fisk
    c. Peter Parker
    d. Stan Lee

> ### Did you know?
> Notice the street sign at Yancy St. This crosses with Stan Lee Blvd. Stan Lee is the creator of Spiderman and a legend in the Marvel universe of characters.

> ### Did you know?
> On the main street you will find the sign for Nelson & Murdock, attorneys at law. This is a reference to the television version of *Daredevil*.

11. ★★ Find the Oscorp building at the corner. Which Marvel villain is seen flying around this building?
    a. Dr. Octopus
    b. Venom
    c. Green Goblin
    d. Jackal

12. ★★★ Find the blue newspaper machine with a copy of The Daily Bugle. According to the front-page article, where did Spiderman and Dr. Octopus have their battle?
    a. Time Square
    b. Central Park
    c. Madison Square Garden
    d. Los Angeles

13. ★★★ What is the name of the boy who is quoted in this article about Spiderman and Dr. Octopus?
    a. Billy Nosegoblin
    b. Billy Hobgoblin
    c. Billy Noseminer
    d. Billy Nosedripper

14. ★ As you walk down the alley towards Doctor Doom's Fearfall, find the banner for Fogwell's Gym. According to the banner, who is not welcome?
    a. Strong
    b. Old
    c. Young
    d. Weak

15. ★ As you read the banner for Fogwell's Gym, which of these is *not* one of the training items listed?
    a. Free weights
    b. Cardio training
    c. Boxing
    d. Strength training

16. ★★★ Find the super hero exchange speaker and press the button. As you hear the message, what is Daredevils real name?
    a. Mark
    b. Maxx
    c. Mitch
    d. Matt

17. ★★★ In the alert from Captain America, which super villain is he calling for all of the Avengers to defeat?
    a. Carney
    b. Carnage
    c. Red Skull
    d. Black Flag

18. ★★★ Which of the X Men does professor Xavier call on through the super hero exchange?
    a. Wolverine
    b. Negasonic Teenage Warhead
    c. Colossus
    d. Deadpool

Doctor Doom's Fearfall

> **Did you know?**
> Before you enter Doctor Doom's Fearfall, stop for a moment to look at the ground just before the entrance. Notice the impact points and outlines of each of the *Fantastic 4* characters.

19. ★ As you walk through the entrance of Doctor Doom's Fearfall, what Marvel universe embassy are you entering?
    a. Doomstadt
    b. Latveria
    c. Symkaria
    d. Madripoor

The Great Universal Studios Orlando Scavenger Hunt

20. ★★ Stop for a moment to read Doctor Doom's code of ethics. What is the Doctor's agenda according to the pledge?
    a. Death to the human race
    b. Revenge
    c. Unlimited power
    d. World domination

Did you know?
After your death defying drop, you will exit through the Arcade. Don't miss a photo opportunity with Doctor Doom's throne.

Did you know?
Take a look around the Arcade, especially the upper corners of the room. Notice the walls are crumbling from the fighting going on around this building.

The Amazing Adventures of Spiderman™

21. ★ As you approach The Amazing Adventures of Spiderman attraction, notice the no parking sign. Between which hours in the morning are you not allowed to park?
    a. 4-7 a.m.
    b. 7-9 a.m.
    c. 9-7 a.m.
    d. 7-4 a.m.

Did you know?
Before you enter the building that houses the Amazing Adventures of Spiderman, take a look at the Express queue sign. It is being held up by a spider web.

22. ★ As you enter the lobby for the Daily Bugle, stop and admire the founders' portrait above you. What is the name of this formidable man?
    a. J. Jonah Jameson
    b. Peter Parker
    c. Eddie Brock
    d. Thomas Fireheart

23. ★★ As you walk through halls of the Daily Bugle, find the newspaper with the headline, "The Doctor Is In". Who is named citizen of the week?
    a. Peter Parker
    b. J. Jonah Jameson
    c. Mary Jane Watson
    d. Minnie the Model

24. ★★ As you read the newspaper with the headline, "Is Spiderman Through?", which member of SHIELD is hailed as an American hero?
    a. Nick Fury
    b. Captain America
    c. Thor of Asgard
    d. Ironman

25. ★★ Find the newspaper with the headline, "Terror from Coast to Coast", which president will be giving a TV speech?
    a. Franklin Delano Roosevelt
    b. Lyndon B. Johnson
    c. Thomas Jefferson
    d. John F. Kennedy

26. ★★★ What volume number is shown on the front page of the Newspaper with the headline, "Terror from Coast to Coast"?
    a. 32, 279
    b. 23,972
    c. 66
    d. 97,232

27. ★★★ Find the newspaper with the headline, "Scream NY Scream!" Where are the foreign ministers meeting to discuss the currency crisis?
    a. New York
    b. London
    c. Paris
    d. Geneva

28. ★★★ In the food section of this newspaper, what did sushi chef Takanohana reveal his secret recipe for?
    a. Green tea ice cream
    b. Squid-beak sashimi
    c. Squid-rollers
    d. Cream-crab rolls

29. ★★ As you enter the first private office, you will find what food item resting on top of a stack of books on the desk?
    a. Croissant
    b. Bagel
    c. Doughnut
    d. An apple

30. ★★ On the wall in red is a sign that reads DEADLINE. What does the line below this word read?
    a. This means your job
    b. Look it up in the dictionary
    c. Get your articles in on time
    d. Time is money

31. ★★ On the poster that reads, "You don't win a Pulitzer by sitting on your _____, so get moving!"
    a. Assci characters
    b. Asses
    c. Headlines
    d. Original news items

32. ★★★ What famous landmark is seen in the framed pictures sitting on the desk just below the sign, "You don't win a Pulitzer by sitting on your"?
    a. The leaning tower of Pisa
    b. The Eiffel tower
    c. The Colosseum
    d. The pyramids of Giza

33. ★★ In the next office, read the blue sign on the wall. What comes last, after get the picture and the story?
    a. Get the facts
    b. Get your story in
    c. Talk to your family
    d. Safety first

34. ★★ What famous landmark is pictured on the calendar you see on the wall in this office?

	a.	The White House	c.	The Statue of Liberty
	b.	The Lincoln Memorial	d.	The Capitol Building

35. ★★★ There is a newspaper on this desk below the wall calendar, which villain is seen on the front page?
    a. Dr. Octopus
    b. Green Goblin
    c. Venom
    d. Doctor Doom

36. ★★★ According to the article from the newspaper on the desk, how much money did this villain abscond with according to the reporter?
    a. 40 million
    b. 45 thousand
    c. 5.4 million
    d. 4.5 million

37. ★★ As you exit the dark room and walk down the hall with the file cabinets, read the archival box #1291-A. What is the topic of this box?
    a. That traitor Spiderman
    b. That pain in the butt Peter Parker
    c. Mary Jane
    d. Green Goblin

38. ★★ As you read the labels on the file cabinets, what name is seen on the label with Betty Brant Leeds?
    a. Stan Lee
    b. Robert Downey Jr.
    c. Captain America
    d. Thor

39. ★★ As you enter your ride vehicle, what does the red sign read as you pass by?
    a. Don't walk
    b. Stop
    c. Don't pass
    d. Wrong way

40. ★★★ As you begin travelling through the city, you will hear the voice of J. Jonah Jameson. What does he say can't be far behind is Spiderman is near?

a.	Safety	c.	Danger
b.	Trouble	d.	Villains

41. ★★ As you catch your first glimpse of Spiderman and he gives you a warning, what does he say at the end of this conversation?
    a. Get out now
    b. You've been warned
    c. Look out for yourselves
    d. Nice shades

42. ★★★ What is the name of the theater you see Spiderman jump onto the marquee?
    a. Marquee
    b. Bijou
    c. Excelsior
    d. Time square

Did you know?

As you exit your ride vehicle, notice J. Jonah Jameson's office above. The anti-gravity machine has been aimed right at his office and Jameson is floating above his desk.

Did you know?

As you were plummeting to your death at the end of the Amazing Adventures of Spiderman, the word UNIVERSAL was spelled out on the manhole cover just before you hit the ground.

Did you know?

As you continue your exploration of Marvel Super Hero Island, notice the bigger than life comic book art surrounding you. It is rumored that when Marvel Super Hero Island was being developed, they designers came to comic book artist Adam Kubert to create this artwork for the park. It is a well-known fact that artists include their name hidden within their sketches. While the rumor states that the park officials asked for the name to be left off, they accidently used the version with Adams name on them. Take some time to search these amazing works of art for Adam's name.

Toon Lagoon

Go back to a simpler time where Cartoons began. Enjoy seeing some of your all-time favorites while you ride with Popeye, Olive Oyl, Dudley Do Right and the rest of the gang.

Adventures await as you join Dudley Do-Right to save Nell from the dastardly Snidely Whiplash. Join Popeye to save Olive Oyl from the mean Bluto.

For guests looking for a bite to eat, try a Dagwood sandwich or eat with your favorite comic strips.

1. ★★ As you enter Toon Lagoon and begin your walk through this island notice the witch that has crashed into a signpost. What is the name of this cartoon witch?
   a. Broom Glinda
   b. Broom Hilda
   c. Hazel
   d. Witchy Poo

2. ★ What is written on the underwear you see this cartoon witch wearing?
   a. Monday
   b. U.S.M.C.
   c. Witch wear
   d. Please return to

3. ★ Stop for a moment in front of Cathy's Ice Cream. What symbol do you see on the front of her swimsuit?

a.	Heart	c.	Club
b.	Spade	d.	Diamond

4. ★★ Find the comic strip for Snuffy Smith. What is it she forgot about next week as you read the frames?
   - a. A bath
   - b. Making dinner
   - c. Choir practice
   - d. Walking the dog

> ### Did you know?
> As you look at the comic for Family Circus, notice the dotted line runs off the page and onto the ground. Feel free to follow the dotted line around to see where it ends.

5. ★★ Notice the speech bubbles around Toon Lagoon. Finish the bubble that says, "If I hear "Say Cheese" again I'll turn into a _____."
   - a. Cheddar
   - b. Gouda
   - c. Monster
   - d. Muenster

6. ★★ Find the fire hydrant with the dogs surrounding it, how many dogs do you see?
   - a. 6
   - b. 7
   - c. 8
   - d. 10

7. ★ What does the dog with his arms stretched out hold in his left hand?
   - a. Another dog
   - b. A beer mug
   - c. A wine glass
   - d. A dog bone

8. ★★ Find the character from Tumbleweed climbing the cactus. What sort of animal is chasing them as they climb to safety?
   - a. Porcupine
   - b. Bear
   - c. Skunk
   - d. Fox

9. ★ What animal do you see sitting atop the Tumbleweeds?
   a. Vulture
   b. Eagle
   c. Swallow
   d. Parrot

10. ★★★ Notice the undertaker off to the side of Tumbleweeds. What is the name of this character whose motto is, "You plug em, I plant em."?
    a. Clem Clodhopper
    b. The Undertaker
    c. Claude Clay
    d. Wart Wimble

Blondies: Home of the Dagwood

11. ★★★ Find Blondies sandwich shop. As you look at the Dagwood sandwich suspended above, which of these is *not* one of the ingredients?
    a. Spaghetti
    b. Lobster
    c. Ham
    d. Peanut butter

> ### Did you know?
> Around the corner from Blondies you will find the comic for Marmaduke. Notice he is running up the building, this is a wonderful picture spot for you to look like Marmaduke is dragging you on his walk.

12. ★★ Step into Blondies and read the comic on the ingredients for the Dagwood sandwich. What does the onion give it?
    a. Brightness
    b. Authority
    c. Tang
    d. Refreshment

13. ★★ What does the pineapple do for the Dagwood sandwich?
    a. Sweetness
    b. Tanginess
    c. Color
    d. Acid

14. ★★ Which of these is *not* one of the tools Dagwood uses to make his sandwich?
    a. Spoon
    b. Drill
    c. Butter knife
    d. Butcher knife

Dudley Do-Right's Ripsaw Falls™

> ### Did you know?
> As you look at the falls for this attraction, notice the faces carved into the mountain. This is a nod to the famed Mount Rushmore in South Dakota with the faces of presidents Washington, Lincoln, Roosevelt and Jefferson

15. ★ As you walk through the queue, you will find a sign for Lamb, Curry and Rice, what is this business?
    a. Restaurant
    b. Taxidermist
    c. Clothing
    d. Attorney

16. ★ Find the poster for The Head Performer. What does Horse hold in his teeth?
    a. Hay
    b. A rose
    c. An Oscar trophy
    d. A blue ribbon

17. ★ As you come to the ticket collection box, what does the writing on the tickets read?
    a. Entry
    b. Void
    c. Admit one
    d. Theater

18. ★ As you read the movie posters, finish this movie title. "Three Men and a _____."
    a. Grizzly
    b. Baby
    c. Girl
    d. Boat

19. ★ What do you see in the cage in the mining area you as you walk through the queue?

	a.	A bird	c.	A mouse
	b.	A bat	d.	A snake

20. ★ As you walk by the dressing room for Dudley Di Right, what was this room originally used for?
    a. Bathroom
    b. Broom closet
    c. Storage room
    d. Snidely Whiplashes dressing room

21. ★★★ As you walk by Nell's dressing room, who is in there with her?
    a. Dudley
    b. Horse
    c. Her father
    d. Snidely Whiplash

22. ★ As you continue exploring the queue, which state outlined do you find hanging on the wall?
    a. North Dakota
    b. South Dakota
    c. Minnesota
    d. Florida

23. ★ Before you get to the load area, you are asked to remove your hat and what other item?
    a. Glasses
    b. Antlers
    c. Mustaches
    d. Coats

> ### Did you know?
> The original cartoon for Dudley Do-right was based on the silent melodrama films of the 1920's. Back in the infancy of films, the characters were caricatures of real people and always overacted on screen.

24. ★★ As you first see the silhouettes of Nell and Snidely Whiplash, what does she call him?
    a. Friend
    b. Villain
    c. Charlatan
    d. Fiend

25. ★ You will see Dudley and Horse inside what sort of boat on the falls above you as you float by?
    a. Canoe
    b. Raft
    c. Sailboat
    d. Rubber Dinghy

26. ★ What is the name of the mine you enter as Snidely tries to crush you with a boulder?
    a. Cantyabe Mine
    b. Bemyvalentine Mine
    c. Wontyabe mine
    d. Yourgonnabe Mine

27. ★★ As you see Snidely Whiplash tying Nell to the railroad tracks, which other character has been tied up also?
    a. Horse
    b. Dudley
    c. George of the Jungle
    d. Super Chicken

28. ★★ As you continue your ride, you hear Dudley say to his horse he's lost what?
    a. His sense of direction
    b. His train of thought
    c. His appetite
    d. Way home

29. ★★ As you pass beneath Dudley and Horse, the sign above says, "Safety first" what is a close second?
    a. Accidents
    b. Danger
    c. Jeopardy
    d. Security

30. ★ As you pass by the advertisement signs, what is Whiplash Lager made from?
    a. Real stuff
    b. Real lager
    c. Real roots
    d. Real logs

31. ★★ What percentage proof is this Whiplash Lager?
    a. 818%
    b. 1178%
    c. 0%
    d. 900%

The Great Universal Studios Orlando Scavenger Hunt

32. ★ When you finish your ride, you arrive at A Lotta Poopoo. What is this place?
    a. Forest
    b. Prison
    c. Volcano
    d. Falls

33. ★★ What sort of forest creature do you see outside of Snidely's prison cell?
    a. Moose
    b. Bear
    c. Squirrel
    d. Beaver

34. ★ What word is written on the bowl in front of Snidely as he shakes his fist at you?
    a. Crow
    b. Dog
    c. Cat
    d. Crook

35. ★ What event is going on today as you pass under the banner?
    a. Wedding ceremony
    b. Award ceremony
    c. Birthday party
    d. Inauguration

Comic Strip Café

36. ★★ Step inside the Comic Strip Café and find the comic for The Better Half. What did he remove from her soup so she can't insult him?
    a. Vowels
    b. Consonants
    c. Punctuation
    d. Quotes

37. ★ Read the conversation bubbles around the food area. Why did they fire the cartoon chef?
    a. He lacked experience
    b. He lacked color
    c. He lacked dimension
    d. He wanted too much money

Catherine F. Olen

38. ★★ Stop and examine the items in the lockers painted on the wall. In the second locker from the left in the top row, which cartoon characters hat do you see?
    a. Yosemite Sam
    b. Boris Badenov
    c. Popeye
    d. The Cat in the Hat

39. ★★ Which classic cartoon character do you see peeking at you from one of the lockers?
    a. Barney
    b. Fievel
    c. Woody Woodpecker
    d. SpongeBob SquarePants

Did you know?

Step out on the patio of The Comic Strip Café and find the Aesop and Son statues. Test the jack hammer next to the column and help with chiseling the wall.

Popeye and Bluto's Bilge-Rat Barges

Did you know?

Popeye appeared for the first time in 1933 on the screen, leaping off the pages of the comic strips. Along with his girlfriend Olive Oyl and nemesis Bluto, they would go on many adventures together, the two men always vying for the hand of Olive.

40. ★ As you begin walking through the queue, stop for a moment at the posters of the crew. What is the name of the cabin boy?
    a. Jeep
    b. Sweet Pea
    c. Popeye
    d. Pluto

The Great Universal Studios Orlando Scavenger Hunt

41. ★★ As you read the notice with Bluto's cruise activities, what is the name of the shuffleboard tournament?
    a. Cannonball
    b. Peg leg
    c. Anchor
    d. Gangplank

42. ★★ What sort of wine tasting can you expect on your cruise under Bluto's cruise activities?
    a. Poison
    b. Briny
    c. Vinegar
    d. Rosey

43. ★ As you read the activities under Popeye's notice, who teaches the hula dancing class?
    a. The Sea Hag
    b. Popeye's mother
    c. Olive Oyl
    d. Sweet Pea

44. ★ Which of these choices is the last item on Popeye's cruise activities?
    a. Mermaid calling
    b. Whale calling
    c. Fish calling
    d. Spinach everything

45. ★★ As you begin your way to the barges, stop for a moment to read the poster for the Sea Witch Hide-out. How many vultures are there on the island?
    a. 1
    b. 237
    c. 327
    d. 732

46. ★ How do you call for help at the complaint office?
    a. Ring the bell
    b. Knock on the door
    c. Yell real loud
    d. Pull the rope

Did you know?

As you walk around the corner from the front of the complaint office, you will notice that every time someone pulls the rope, a match lights the fuse of the cannon pointed at the door.

47. ★ As you step into Bluto's office, what shape adorns the wallpaper in the office?
    a. Anchors
    b. Sailboats
    c. Cannons
    d. Rafts

48. ★ What did Bluto win the award for that you see resting on the shelf?
    a. Captain of the year
    b. Sucker of the year
    c. Bad guy of the year
    d. Brute of the year

49. ★ You will see a dollar bill on the wall, what is the significance of this dollar?
    a. First dollar earned
    b. First dollar stolen
    c. First dollar printed
    d. First dollar destroyed

> ### Did you know?
> As you look around Bluto's office, notice the cannon in the room. This cannon has blown a hole in the wall and part of the dart board he had Popeye's picture pinned to.

50. ★★ Continue your way through the queue until you come to several noticed posted on the wall. According to Bluto's sailing tips, what do you do if your boat sinks?
    a. Grab a life vest
    b. Grab a passing sea turtle
    c. Grab a bar of soap
    d. Grab your butt and swim

51. ★★ As you read some of the letters pinned to the wall, why didn't Slag beat Bluto?
    a. He's a good friend
    b. He's out of town
    c. He can't find Bluto
    d. He's sick

The Great Universal Studios Orlando Scavenger Hunt

52. ★★ The sea hag wrote in her letter, "Even your _____ was high."
    a. Captain
    b. First mate
    c. Anchor
    d. Tide

53. ★★★ Which of the characters can't spell S.O.S.?
    a. The Sea Hag
    b. Patcheye the Pirate
    c. Jabbo
    d. Slag

54. ★ As you approach the luggage drop area, what is the name of the parrot that is the mascot for Bluto's Bilge-Rat Barges?
    a. Polly
    b. Olive
    c. Salty
    d. Jenny

55. ★★★ As you read the chalkboard with the sailing times, which cruise took the longest time?
    a. Low seas
    b. High seas
    c. Sweetheaven tours
    d. Jeep island

56. ★ What is the title of the beige book lying on its side on the shelf of the luggage office?
    a. Lumber Jack Love
    b. The Gentle Lover
    c. Mom Gravy
    d. Lumber Jack Jim

57. ★★ As you begin making your way to the load area, look up at the rafters around you. What very unusual items do you see that doesn't seem to go with a cruise?
    a. Turkey feathers
    b. Hot water bottles
    c. Bowling pins
    d. Bombs

58. ★ Just before you board, read the sign warning that you will get wet. What name do they use to refer to the people taking this cruise?
    a. Landlord
    b. Landlover
    c. Landlubber
    d. Land dweller

59. ★★ As you begin your cruise, notice the sign under the first bridge. What kind of food can you get to go?
    a. Fish & chips
    b. Fish sandwich
    c. Burgers
    d. Squid sandwich

60. ★ Along your way, watch out for Popeye and Bluto pulling on something they are fighting over. What is this item?
    a. Can of spinach
    b. Olive Oyl
    c. A bag of money
    d. The ships wheel

61. ★ Which giant sea creature is sweet pea climbing on to retrieve a can of spinach?
    a. Octopus
    b. Squid
    c. Whale
    d. Kraken

62. ★★ What is the name of Bluto's boat?
    a. S.S. Bluto
    b. S.S. Badguy
    c. S.S. Stinker
    d. S.S. Popeye sucks

—∽—

63. ★ As you continue your way through Cartoon Lagoon, find Gasoline Alley. how many tires do you see stacked up outside the service station?
    a. Eight
    b. Ten
    c. Five
    d. Eighty

64. ★★★ Outside of Wossamotta U store, you will see the silhouettes of characters on top of the stadium. Which character do you see to the far left on the stadium?
    a. Sherman
    b. Snidely Whiplash
    c. Mr. Peabody
    d. Rocky J. Squirrel

Did you know?

On the road through Toon Lagoon you will find a large red Hush A Bomb. Pull the plunger and push it down quickly to detonate the bomb.

Skull Island: Reign of Kong

Go on an adventure to a strange island where time stands still. Do you have the courage to come face to face with the greatest beast known to man? Find out on Skull Island.

> **Did you know?**
> As you enter the queue for Skull Island: Reign of Kong notice the archway above you has the shape of King Kong's head.

1. ★★ As you enter the queue, find the table with the radio equipment. What is stored in the small red container on the table?
   a. Tobacco
   b. Tea
   c. Coffee
   d. Nuts

2. ★ Read the label on the wooden crate next to the table. Which of these is the correct wording on the label?
   a. Seventh Wonder
   b. Tenth Wonder
   c. Eighth Wonder
   d. Eightieth Wonder

> ### Did you know?
> As you walk through the queue for Skull Island: Reign of Kong, you will see a native shaman chanting. If you are in this room long enough you will experience the screeching of spirits and the flames growing brighter.

3. ★ Just before entering your transport vehicle, what sort of creature do you find beneath the glass encasement moving around?
   a. Bird
   b. Tortoise
   c. Badger
   d. Worm

4. ★★ Before you enter your transport, read the labels on the crates around you. What is the packed date on the 50 lbs. of TNT?
   a. October 23, 1939
   b. October 29, 1923
   c. October 23, 1929
   d. October 17, 1929

5. ★★ Find the chalkboard with the notes for each transport. What does the chart state is Kalana's task?
   a. Investigate native sightings
   b. Capture V-Rex bait
   c. Photo reconnaissance
   d. Examine skeletal remains

6. ★★ Which driver is missing according to the chalkboard chart?
   a. Jared
   b. Doc
   c. Becky
   d. Will

Catherine F. Olen

> ### Did you know?
> If you have the chance, take a look at the driver of your transport vehicle. The driver seems to be rather stiff and mannequin like, wouldn't you say?
>
> A fun piece of trivia about this attraction: each driver you see has a different voice over on the ride. If you ride Kong: Skull Island more than once, you will hear different drivers depending on which transport you ride on.

7. ★★ If you listen closely, the radio conversation will tell you why you are on this transport. Which is the correct reason for your journey?
   a. Save the team
   b. Capture King Kong
   c. Replacement supplies
   d. Supply team with weapons

8. ★★ As the massive gates open, what word do you hear the natives chanting?
   a. No
   b. Kong
   c. Sacrifice
   d. Go back

9. ★ As you enter the cave, what prehistoric creatures do you see alongside the transport vehicle?
   a. Dinosaurs
   b. Apes
   c. Birds
   d. Bats

10. ★ As you find the group in the cave, what does Joe use to create more light?
    a. Torches
    b. Fire pit
    c. Flare gun
    d. Glow sticks

11. ★★★ Along your journey you will encounter dinosaurs that attack your transport. What species of dinosaur do you see?
    a. Tyrannosaurus Rex
    b. Pterodactyl
    c. Velociraptor
    d. Apatosaurus

> ### Did you know?
> As you watch Kong protecting you from the dinosaurs be sure to look back over your left shoulder to see the dinosaur drag the transport following you down the canyon just before you fall too.

12. ★★ As you come face to face with Kong, what entity does the driver ask for protection?
    a. Gods
    b. Gorilla
    c. Shamans
    d. Spirits

Jurassic Park

Explore a world where Dinosaurs roam free among the guests of Islands of Adventure. Get up close and personal with the experts or ride down the river to see history come alive right before your eyes.

For the truly brave, meet one of the deadliest dinosaurs that has ever walked the earth face to face.

Join the scientists as they breed a new generation of dinosaurs. Be there to watch a newly hatched dinosaur and maybe even pet a baby.

> ### Did you know?
> As you wander through the Jurassic Park area of Islands of Adventure, look at the pavement beneath your feet. You will see plant fossils scattered throughout the area.

Jurassic Park River Adventure

1. ☆ As you enter your boat and begin the ascent to the river, read the warning sign to your left. Which of these is *not* one of the items listed on the warning sign?
    a. Feeding
    b. Eating
    c. Yelling
    d. Flash Photography

2. ★★ As your narrator begins speaking, what is the ever-changing river he refers to?
   a. History
   b. Earth
   c. Dinosaurs
   d. Time

3. ★★ Which of the dinosaur species is the most primitive of the horned dinosaurs?
   a. Psittacosaurus
   b. Stegosaurus
   c. Diloposaurus
   d. Parasaurolophus

4. ★★ As your cruise begins to go astray, which gate do you go through to enter the Raptor containment area?
   a. 15
   b. 3
   c. 13
   d. 31

5. ★ As you enter the warehouse, you will notice a sign in the window of the control room to your left. What does this sign read?
   a. Be careful
   b. Be attentive
   c. Behave
   d. Be alert

6. ★★ As you explore the Jurassic Park area, find the triceratops fossil. What does the name Triceratops mean?
   a. Three-horn face
   b. Two-horn face
   c. Three-horned monster
   d. Three-toed animal

Jurassic Park Discovery Center

Did you know?

As you wander through the Jurassic Park Discovery Center, be sure to keep an eye out for the famed Barbasol can that was used to transport embryo's in the first *Jurassic Park* film.

7. ★★ What type of dietary supplement do you find next to the Barbasol can in the supply room?
   a. L-Carnitine
   b. L-Lysine
   c. L-Glutamine
   d. L-Tyrosine

8. ★★ On the shelf just below the Barbasol can, what sort of gun case do you see?
   a. Pistol
   b. Shot gun
   c. Tranquilizer gun
   d. Stun gun

9. ★★ As you continue your tour of the nursery, what company manufactures the dinosaur eggs?
   a. Millipore
   b. Dinopore
   c. Maxipore
   d. Tiranipore

10. ★★ How do the bioengineers at the discovery center soften the egg shells to make hatching easier on the baby dinosaurs?
    a. Warm water bath
    b. Chemical wash
    c. Boiling
    d. Gas wash

Did you know?

If you are in the discovery center, keep an eye out for the opportunity to see a baby dinosaur being hatched right before your eyes. If you are the lucky visitor, you can even name the new life at Jurassic Park and receive a certificate commemorating the event.

Did you know?

Keep an eye out for the Jurassic Park scientists walking through the center with a baby dinosaur for you to interact with at various times throughout the day.

Camp Jurassic

> **Did you know?**
> The entrance sign to Camp Jurassic is made of dinosaur fossils.

11. ★ Find the Welcome to camp Jurassic sign. Which of these is *not* one of the items listed for you to do?
    a. Discover
    b. Rock Climbing
    c. Slide
    d. Explore

> **Did you know?**
> Camp Jurassic hides the entrance to the Pterodactyl Flyers attraction, the only attraction at Islands of Adventure that requires a child in order to ride.

> **Did you know?**
> As you explore Camp Jurassic, you may stumble upon caverns where you will find raw amber with mosquitos within. Be careful or you may be sprayed by the underground geysers within these caverns.

> **Did you know?**
> Hidden in the brush of Jurassic Park, you will find the entrance to the Raptor Encounter. Keep your head up as you never know what could be hunting you.

The Wizarding World of Harry Potter™ - Hogsmeade

As you enter the magical mystical world of Harry Potter, you will explore the well-known shops and attractions that bring you right to the heart of the Harry Potter™ books. Become a wizard yourself when you don your robes, hold your wand in hand and transport yourself to a world where anything is possible.

Fly on a broom as you explore Hogwarts™ Castle or meet a Hippogriff on an exciting rollercoaster.

Join Hagrid as you explore the magical creatures that are his best friends. Be sure to visit the wand master at Ollivanders™ to get your new wand before your time in Hogsmeade is through.

1. ★★ As you enter Hogsmeade, stop before the window of Zonko's Joke Shop and look at the window above. In what year was McHavelock's Hats and Wigs established?
    a. 1687   c. 1786
    b. 1867   d. 1768

2. ★★ Find the 3-D Dr. Filibuster in the window. What sort of eye wear is he wearing?

a. Eyeglasses c. Contact lenses
b. Opera glasses d. Monocle

> **Did you know?**
> Watch the wizard's chess piece in the window of Zonko's. They move and destroy each other every few seconds.

3. ★ Find the girl puking into the bucket in the window of Zonko's Joke Shop. What is the name of the product she is advertising?
   a. Puking Pastilles c. Puking Patterns
   b. Puking Pastries d. Puking Pudding

4. ★★ On the eves of Zonko's you will see descriptions of what they sell inside. Which of these is *not* one of the items listed?
   a. Jokes c. Tricks
   b. Games d. Sweets

Honeydukes™

5. ★★ Around the top of the room inside Honeydukes, you will find pink swirl lollypops. How many do you find in Honeydukes?
   a. 10 c. 16
   b. 34 d. 52

6. ★ Honeydukes sells what sort of pink coconut candy?
   a. Suckers c. Fudge
   b. Cotton candy d. Ice

7. ★★★ In the alley behind Honeydukes, you will find a window with a candy display. Find the jar with red gummies candies. What sort of creatures are these candies made to look like?

a. Bears
c. Frogs
b. Wands
d. Snakes

> **Did you know?**
>
> Between Zonko's and Honeydukes you will find the doorway for McHavelock's Wizarding Headgear. The cauldron above, with a wave of your interactive wand, will tip forward and reveal a pixie.

8. ★★ Across the road you will find the Hogwarts's Express for picture opportunities. The time table shows you what time the Hogwarts Express will leave the station. In the lower right corner is the timetable for Saturday/Sunday and what other special day?
   a. Christmas
   c. Boxing day
   b. Halloween
   d. Easter

9. ★★ As you read the time table, what is the first fare from Cardiff to Kingly Langley on Tuesday?
   a. 50.00
   c. 69.45
   b. 62.50
   d. 45.69

10. ★★ According to the Hogsmeade timetable, what is the date of registration of this document?
    a. 24 February
    c. 30 November
    b. 24 December
    d. 31 December

Three Broomsticks™

> **Did you know?**
>
> As you enter The Three Broomsticks, look around you at the walls. Notice fairies and elves appearing in shadows around you throughout the room every so often.

11. ★★★ Throughout the Three Broomsticks you will find antlers displayed. How many total antlers are there displayed within this restaurant?
    a. 26
    b. 36
    c. 16
    d. 63

Hog's Head™ Pub

12. ★ Which one of these is on the chalk board for yesterday's specials at Hogs Head Pub?
    a. Steak and Kidney Pudding
    b. Steak and Kidney Pie
    c. Kipper Pudding
    d. Kipper Pie

13. ★★ As you look around this room, read the sign directing you how to leave after what hour?
    a. The witching hour
    b. Closing time
    c. Midnight
    d. Morning

> **Did you know?**
> Notice the hogs head behind the bar. Watch carefully for him to move his head side to side and snort his displeasure at the patrons.

14. ★ How many shrunken heads do you find behind the bar at the Hogs Head Pub?
    a. 3
    b. 4
    c. 5
    d. 1

15. ★★ What does the warning sign behind the bar remind you not to lose?
    a. Your wallet
    b. Your head
    c. Your wand
    d. Your lunch

Catherine F. Olen

> **Did you know?**
> Find the stairs next to the bar in the Hog's Head. Listen carefully and you can hear the house elves on the second floor actively taking care of guests.

16. ★ Step outside and continue your exploration of Hogsmeade. Based on the clues around you, what time of year it is?
    a. Spring
    b. Summer
    c. Fall
    d. Winter

> **Did you know?**
> Look at the water pump and drinking trough outside the Hog's Head Pub. The water is frozen solid in the trough as well as frozen coming out of the spout.

> **Did you know?**
> Find the store front for Dogweed and Deathcap Exotic Plants and Flowers. Make sure you have your earmuffs as you will see a mandrake in the window.

17. ★★★ Find the window for J. Pippins Potions. If you look very carefully in this second story window, find the clear bottle with the white label. What does this bottle contain?
    a. Gillyweed
    b. Fluxweed
    c. Screechsnap
    d. Snakeweed

> ### Did you know?
> Find the restrooms, known as conveniences, in this area of Hogsmeade. Listen carefully and you will hear Moaning Myrtle terrorizing the unsuspecting guests who use the potties in Hogsmeade.

18. ☆ Continue your exploration of Hogsmeade and enter the covered area just outside the Owl Post. As you stand under the eaves and look directly above you, what animals do you see resting in the eaves?
    a. Eagles
    b. Owls
    c. Rats
    d. Toads

> ### Did you know?
> The designers were so detailed in their representation of Hogsmeade they even included bird droppings on the perches.

Dervish and Banges™

19. ☆ Find the cage in the center of Dervish and Banges that holds the Monster Book of Monsters. What does the warning sign say it might do to you?
    a. Growl at you
    b. Escape
    c. Bite you
    d. Tear up your books

20. ☆☆☆ On the second floor of Dervish and Banges find several boxes of Lowdour stacked up. What is this product according to the label?
    a. Love potion
    b. Deodorant
    c. Face powder
    d. Hair cream

21. ★★ Sitting atop one of the display cases you will find the Tri-wizards cup. Who won this prize in 1943?
    a. Margot Droope
    b. Angelus Moriattis
    c. Stephan Hodhedge
    d. Dominic Maestro

22. ★★ Next to the cup for the Quaffle Control you will find a stack of books on their side. Finish this title, "_____ from across the world?
    a. Owl breeds
    b. Famous wizards
    c. Lesser known muggles
    d. Famous frogs

23. ★★ Behind the counter you will find a framed notice for closing procedures. What does number 7 tell you to do?
    a. Escort out remaining customers
    b. Lock all doors
    c. Double check the lock on the Monster Book of Monsters
    d. Cast a security spell

Did you know?

Look at the second floor of Dervish and Banges and you will see several brooms tied to the rail so they cannot fly away. Notice as they sway as they wait for their wizards to return for them.

Owl Post

Did you know?

If you mail your letters and postcards from the owl post, you will receive a Hogsmeade postmark. This is a wonderful souvenir of your time in the wizard realm.

The Great Universal Studios Orlando Scavenger Hunt

24. ★★★ In the window, you will see several packages wrapped in brown paper waiting to be shipped. Which wizarding item do you see outlined in its wrapper?
    a. Magic wand
    b. Cloak of invisibility
    c. Witches hat
    d. Crystal ball

> **Did you know?**
>
> As you look around the Owl Post, you will see several owls on their perches ready to fly to their destinations, watch as their heads turn, and notice the droppings on their perches.

25. ★★★ On the side of Owl Post you will find several packages stacked up in the window. Watch as a howler appears and tells you that you have arrived in Hogsmeade without what?
    a. Permission form
    b. Enchantment
    c. Broom
    d. Wand

26. ★★★ According to the howler that appears outside Dervish and Banges, what kind of ball did you practice Quidditch with?
    a. Golden snitch
    b. Golden
    c. Crystal
    d. Rubber

Gladrags Wizardwear

27. ★★ Look in the window of Gladrags and you will see a measuring tape in the shape of what animal?
    a. A turkey
    b. A cat
    c. A frog
    d. An owl

28. ★ According to the sign in the door window, why is this shop closed?
    a. Out fitting
    b. On a break
    c. Ran out of cloth
    d. Wizarding holiday

Catherine F. Olen

Scrivenshaft's Finest Parchment, Ink and Quills

29. ★★★ Peek in the window of Scrivenshaft's and you will see a sewing machine in the center of the room. Which brand sewing machine do you see?
    a. Atlas
    b. Betsy Ross
    c. Bernina
    d. Singer

> **Did you know?**
> As you look around the shop, notice the quill writing in the ledger without the help of a clerk.

Madam Puddifoot's

30. ★ In the window of Madam Puddifoot's you will see a three-tier cake. What shape are the layers of this lovely cake?
    a. Round
    b. Square
    c. Heart
    d. Hexagon

31. ★ Notice in Madam Puddifoot's the hundreds of tea cups scattered around. How many are dangling from hooks on the shelves in the back of the shop?
    a. 16
    b. 26
    c. 76
    d. 116

32. ★★ As you continue looking in the window of Madam Puddifoot's find the cake with the bunny on the top. What sort of flowers do you see on the sides of this cake?
    a. Roses
    b. Sunflowers
    c. Peonies
    d. Birds of Paradise

33. ★★ Notice the brightly colored eggs on the top of this cake? How many eggs do you see?

a. 10 c. 11
b. 12 d. 7

Ceridwen's Cauldron

34. ★★ Outside of Ceridwen's Cauldron you will see a large stack of cauldrons waiting for owners. How many cauldrons do you see?
    a. 8 c. 12
    b. 72 d. 17

Tomes and Scrolls Specialist Bookshop

35. ★ In what year was Tomes and Scrolls Specialist Bookshop established?
    a. 1678 c. 1968
    b. 1768 d. 1876

36. ★★ As you look in the window of Tomes and Scrolls, notice several books by famed wizard Gilderoy Lockhart. Which of these titles is *not* in the window?
    a. *Meandering with Mummies*
    b. *Year with a Yeti*
    c. *Travels with Trolls*
    d. *Break with a Banshee*

37. ★★★ Find the book *Beedle the Bard* in the window display. Who is the illustrator of this wizarding book?
    a. Mary GrandPre c. Luxos Karuzos
    b. Andrew Davidson d. Gilderoy Lockhart

38. ★★★ As you watch wizards waves their wand at the book *Beedle the Bard*, the book magically opens to reveal the text within. Finish this line, "High on a hill in an enchanted _____."
    a. Castle c. Room
    b. Fortress d. Garden

39. ★★★ What is the name of the fountain enclosed by tall walls?
    a. Dark magic
    b. Youth
    c. Fair fortune
    d. Earthly riches

40. ★★★ Find the typewriter surrounded by books. What is the brand of typewriter?
    a. Remington
    b. Royal
    c. Lillian Rose
    d. Torpedo

> **Did you know?**
> On the shelf you will find a small blue book with the title *Quality Street* by author J.M. Barrie. J.M. Barrie is best known for writing the children's classic *Peter Pan*.

Flight of the Hippogriff™

41. ★ As you walk through the line for Flight of the Hippogriff, what sort of vegetable does Hagrid grow in his garden?
    a. Watermelons
    b. Corn
    c. Green beans
    d. Pumpkins

> **Did you know?**
> As you walk through Hagrid's garden, notice his scarecrow is wearing a Hogwarts robe.

42. ★★★ Listen carefully as you approach Hagrid's shack. What warning do you hear him giving?

a. The forest is forbidden to all students
b. The spiders will kill you
c. Do not mess with Mr. Filch
d. Draco Malfoy is going to cause you trouble

Did you know?
Listen carefully as you walk by Hagrid's hut, you can hear Fang barking at the strangers invading his house.

Bonus question

43. ★★★ As you walk by Hagrid's, you will see his motorbike parked outside. Which Harry Potter character owned this bike before Hagrid?
    a. Lord Voldemort
    b. James Potter
    c. Sirius Black
    d. Professor Dumbledore

44. ★ As you walk by Hagrid's hut you will see a crate that once contained a baby dragon. Which breed of dragon was held in this crate?
    a. Romanian Longhorn
    b. Norwegian Ridgeback
    c. Hungarian Horntail
    d. Peruvian Vipertooth

Ollivanders™

45. ★ As you stand in front of Ollivanders, in what year was this wand shop established?
    a. 382 BC
    b. 832 BC
    c. 382 AD
    d. 832 AD

46. ★ As you watch the wand fitting, how is the wizard fitted for their wand?
    a. The wand chooses the wizard
    b. By the length of the wand
    c. The wizard chooses the wand
    d. Go to the giftshop

47. ★★ As the wand fitter tells you about Ollivanders, which of these is *not* one of the items used in a wand core?
    a. Unicorn hair
    b. Dragon Heartstring
    c. Phoenix tail feather
    d. Hippogriff Tailfeather

> **Did you know?**
>
> As the wand fitter gives the selected customer the wands, if the wand is not a good fit for this person some very unusual things will happen. Keep an eye out for strange goings on around the room.

48. ★★ As the wand fitter finds the correct wand for the customer, what warning does he give on how to store your wands?
    a. Never store it in the cold
    b. Never store it in your locker
    c. Never store it in your back pocket
    d. Never lend your wand to another wizard

Harry Potter and the Forbidden Journey™

49. ★★ As you enter the dungeon of Hogwarts castle, one of the first things you see is the Mirror of Erised. What word is seen at the very top point of the mirror?
    a. Out
    b. Ube
    c. Ehru
    d. Erised

The Great Universal Studios Orlando Scavenger Hunt

> ### Did you know?
> The Mirror of Erised shows the deepest darkest desire of your heart. Did you notice the words around the mirror say, "I show not your face but your heart's desire" spelled backwards?

50. ★★★ Stop for a moment at the door for the potion's classroom. Which Hogwarts student is being tutored as you listen through the door?
    a. Harry
    b. Ron
    c. Neville
    d. Draco

> ### Did you know?
> As you enter the Herbology area notice the small area to the right of the castle entrance with several kinds of plants. As you walk by, be sure to take notice of the baby mandrakes in the clay pots.

51. ★ As you enter the castle, notice the statue of the architect of Hogwarts castle. What does he hold in his left hand?
    a. A scroll
    b. A castle
    c. A key
    d. A wand

52. ★★ As you enter the castle, you will see the hourglasses for the house points. As you look at the hourglasses, which house is winning?
    a. Hufflepuff
    b. Slytherin
    c. Ravenclaw
    d. Gryffindor

Catherine F. Olen

> ### Did you know?
> At the end of this hall you will see a large statue of a bird. This is the secret entrance to the office of Albus Dumbledore, head master of Hogwarts.

53. ★★ As you enter the portrait hall, you will see portraits of the four founders of Hogwarts. As they talk back and forth about Hagrid losing a Dragon, which building do they hope will not get burned down again?
    a. The chapel
    b. The owlery
    c. Herbology
    d. Hagrid's hut

54. ★★ One of the Hogwarts founders says this sounds like a clear violation of the warlock convention of what year?
    a. 1709
    b. 1907
    c. 1207
    d. 1509

55. ★★ Which of the four portraits detests muggles entering Hogwarts school?
    a. Godric Gryffindor
    b. Helga Hufflepuff
    c. Rowena Ravenclaw
    d. Salazar Slytherin

56. ★★ As you approach Dumbledore's office, he will greet you and talk about the students of Hogwarts. He says some have strayed where?
    a. The haunted forest
    b. The dark side
    c. The death eaters
    d. The village of Hogsmeade

57. ★★ What is Tom Riddle known as these days according to Dumbledore?
    a. Tom Riddle
    b. Severus Snape
    c. Lord Voldemort
    d. Harry Potter

58. ★★ Dumbledore tells you there comes a time in everyone's life when they must make a choice between what is right and what?
   a. What is evil
   b. What is wrong
   c. Being lazy
   d. What is easy

59. ★★ How long will the hundreds of years of Hogwarts history be condensed down to according to Dumbledore?
   a. A few short hours
   b. A few short days
   c. A few short minutes
   d. A few short years

> **Did you know?**
> As you walk through the office of Albus Dumbledore, look closely and you will find the pensieve Harry Potter used to look at people's memories.

60. ★ How do Ron, Hermione and Harry enter the defense against the dark arts classroom?
   a. Walked in
   b. Flew in on brooms
   c. Waved their wands
   d. Cloak of invisibility

61. ★★ What does Hermione say to you about the history of Hogwarts?
   a. It's boring
   b. It's fascinating
   c. It's long
   d. It's light reading

62. ★★ What do Harry, Ron, and Hermione invite you to do?
   a. Go for a bite to eat
   b. See a play
   c. See a game of Quidditch
   d. Sneak into the dark forest

63. ★★ What happens to the classroom as the trio are chatting with you?
   a. You hear thunder
   b. A lightning strike
   c. The sun comes out
   d. It starts snowing

64. ★★★ Stop to read the black board in the defense against the dark arts classroom. What do dementors force victims to do according to the writing on the board?
    a. Relive your childhood
    b. Relive your worst memories
    c. Believe you can't accomplish your dreams
    d. Make you forget your family

65. ★★★ To cast the Patronus charm, think of a single what according to the blackboard?
    a. Happy memory
    b. Thing you like
    c. Happy little thought
    d. Person you want to help

66. ★★ The skeleton of what creature hovers above you in the defense against the dark arts classroom?
    a. Unicorn
    b. Dragon
    c. Spider
    d. Owl

> **Did you know?**
>
> As you enter the student common room, look for the table with the stack of books on it. Notice a Defense Against the Dark Arts book sitting on the table?

67. ★ As you enter the common room, you will see a bowl of what sort of fruit?
    a. Oranges
    b. Figs
    c. Apples
    d. Bananas

68. ★★ On the top of the cabinet you will find a game board for which game?
    a. Chess
    b. Parcheesi
    c. Secrets
    d. Backgammon

The Great Universal Studios Orlando Scavenger Hunt

> **Did you know?**
> As you walk through the common room you will hear the portraits above talking about the ride vehicles you will be flying on. Enjoy their bickering back and forth as they educate you on your ride.

69. ★ As you come to the sorting hat, you must be taller than what size to ride this attraction?
    a. Goblin
    b. Troll
    c. Pixie
    d. Dragon

70. ★ The sorting hat advises you to put your belongings in lockers that are enchanted to protect from what?
    a. Dementor
    b. Death eater
    c. Wizard
    d. Magic

71. ★ Which student of Hogwarts creates the enchantment so your ride will fly?
    a. Harry
    b. Hermione
    c. Ron
    d. Hagrid

72. ★ What does Hagrid hold up when he asks you if you have seen a dragon?
    a. A rope
    b. A dragon egg
    c. A wand
    d. A metal chain and collar

> **Did you know?**
> As the dragon is chasing you around the castle, did you notice the dragon claw marks along the roof just before he appears?

73. ★★ What does Hermione warn you to watch out for after she saves you from the spiders?
    a. The Whomping Willow
    b. The dementors
    c. The death eaters
    d. The quidditch pit

74. ★ After your daring escape from the dementors, where does Harry tell you to go?
    a. The tower
    b. The Gryffindor common room
    c. The Great Hall
    d. Dumbledore's office

75. ★★★ Which of these choices is *not* one of the challenges you faced on Harry Potter and the Forbidden Journey?
    a. Dementors
    b. Dragon
    c. The Whomping Willow
    d. Lord Voldemort

> ### Did you know?
> Do not miss the opportunity to ride The Hogwarts Express from Hogsmeade to Diagon Alley on the Universal side of the theme parks.

The Lost Continent

Explore the ancient ruins of Poseidon's lair and save the world from evil. Dine in the ruins of an ancient civilization and then spend some time chatting with the enchanted fountain on The Lost Continent.

> **Did you know?**
> Stand before Mythos Restaurant. While this restaurant boasted some of the finest cuisine at Islands of Adventure, take some time to marvel at the spectacular architecture inside and outside of this hidden gem in The Lost Continent.

Poseidon's Fury: Escape from the Lost City

1. ★ Look high above you at the ruin of the statue of Poseidon at the entrance to Poseidon's Fury: Escape from the Lost City. What object does he hold in his hand?
   a. Pitchfork
   b. Trident
   c. Triton
   d. Magic wand

2. ★ What sea creature appears on the large broken emblem above the entrance to Poseidon's Fury?
   a. Crab
   b. Whale
   c. Octopus
   d. Clam

3. ★★ As you read the journal left behind by the Global Discovery Group, how many years ago was the Temple of Poseidon constructed?
   a. 2000 years
   b. 20000 years
   c. 200 years
   d. 3000 years

4. ★★ As you continue reading the writings left behind in the temple, what was the only group allowed within the temple of Poseidon?
   a. Sea creatures
   b. Priests of the Inner Circle
   c. Oceanic royalty
   d. Poseidon's family

5. ★★ As you see the archeologist come in the room where you are standing, what does he call this room?
   a. The chamber of doom
   b. The chamber of Poseidon
   c. The chamber of the forbidden eye
   d. The chamber of sacrifice

6. ★★ What is the name of the archeologist Taylor works for?
   a. Professor Jones
   b. Professor Orlando
   c. Professor Baxter
   d. Professor Poseidon

7. ★★ What is the name of the evil God who killed everyone as a sacrifice to the evil one?
   a. Darkanon
   b. Darkness
   c. Donnie Dark
   d. Dangerous One

8. ★★ As Taylor reads the secret message, what object do you need to find to restore peace?
   a. Poseidon's trident
   b. The secret chamber
   c. Poseidon
   d. Darkanon

9. ★★ As the doors open to the secret chamber, what does the voice tell you to step into?
   a. Your doom
   b. Your destiny
   c. Your death
   d. Your Life

10. ★★ When Taylor comments about the spiderwebs, what does he say looks like it threw up?
    a. A spider family
    b. Spiders from Harry Potter
    c. All the spiders of the world
    d. Spiderman

> ### Did you know?
> The attraction Poseidon's Fury: Escape from the Lost City is a walk-through attraction with many hidden special effects through dark passageways. You will find several platforms within each room allowing all guest to see each part of the show with ease.

11. ★ When Taylor finds the trident, who does he summon into the chamber?
    a. The Gods
    b. Poseidon
    c. The Goddess
    d. The exit

12. ★★ Why is it beyond the goddess' power to grant you passage back to your world?

- a. Her magic has been taken
- b. There are no exits in this chamber
- c. Darkanon has taken her prisoner
- d. Locking spell impervious to magic

13. ⭐⭐ As you listen to the Goddess, she explains that she can grant you what?
    - a. Safe passage back where you came from
    - b. Safe passage deeper into the temple
    - c. An audience with Poseidon
    - d. A protection spell against Darkanon

Did you know?

As you watch the wall move back it reveals a tunnel, you will see that it is a water tunnel with the water swirling around you. This water moves at over one hundred miles per hour without the aid of a tube. As you begin your walk through, you will feel the water spray. Even though you can touch the water, you can be injured due to the velocity as is moves around the tunnel.

Did you know?

As you come through the tunnel, you find yourself in yet another small room with a doorway. While Taylor attempts to open the door, he fails until Poseidon helps him. The room goes dark to reveal a huge chamber. This effect is done with false walls surrounding you that are removed in the darkness to see the full scope of the chamber once the light resumes.

The Great Universal Studios Orlando Scavenger Hunt

14. ★★ You find yourself in the Chamber of Poseidon. What sea creature do you see swimming as the light in the room becomes brighter?
    a. Octopus
    b. Whale
    c. Dolphin
    d. Schools of fish

15. ★★ As Darkanon fights Poseidon for power, how long ago did he say their battle began?
    a. Hundreds of years ago
    b. A thousand years ago
    c. A thousand millennia ago
    d. A million years ago

> ### Did you know?
> Throughout the Lost Continent area, you will find small shops with custom jewelry, clothing and artwork. Be sure to spend time within these shops during your time on the Lost Continent.

> ### Did you know?
> As you walk from the Lost Continent towards Seuss Landing, you will cross a wooden bridge. If you look towards the water, you will notice a smaller bridge closer to the waters edge. If you travel down the path and cross this small bridge, you will hear the troll that lives under the bridge.

Seuss Landing

Enter the pages of your favorite childhood stories when you walk through the gates of Seuss Landing.

Ride with the Sneetches or go to the playground with the animals from *If I Ran the Zoo*. When you get hungry, stop off for some *Green Eggs and Ham* and finish the day with *The Cat in the Hat*, but be sure to clean up before your mother gets home.

1. ★★ As you enter Seuss Landing from Hogsmeade, one of the first things you find is the Moose Juice store. Find the poem, "Happy Birthday to You" and finish this line, "Thank goodness I'm not just a clam or a ham or a dusty old jar of _____ jam."
    a. Sour Seusselberry jam
    b. Tart pineapple jam
    c. Sweet boysenberry jam
    d. Sour gooseberry jam

2. ★★ Look in the windows of Honk Honkers and you will find a yellow birthday cake. How many candles are on this cake?
    a. Six
    b. Seven
    c. Eight
    d. Ten

The Great Universal Studios Orlando Scavenger Hunt

3. ★ As you walk along the path you will find a lamppost with a sign hanging down. What lives in the lamp?
   a. Cramp
   b. Zamp
   c. Stamp
   d. Tramp

Mulberry Street Store, Gizmo's, Gadgets, Goodies Galore

4. ★ As you look up at the front of the Mulberry Street Store, you will find two matching characters from this beloved book on the roof. What animal do you see?
   a. Zebra
   b. Horse
   c. Giraffe
   d. Elephant

5. ★★ As you enter the Mulberry Street Store, look for the Who's Asleep score. Which of these is the correct score?
   a. 70500 zillion
   b. 70500 billion
   c. 70500 million
   d. 75000 zillion

6. ★★ Find the gauge with the three purple hands. Which of these is *not* one of the numbers you see on this gauge?
   a. 133
   b. 721
   c. 30
   d. 472

7. ★★ Find the blue clock sitting in an alcove. What is the correct time on this clock?
   a. 4:55
   b. 5:55
   c. 5:05
   d. 2:35

Did you know?

As you walk along the path through Seuss Landing, you will find a grandstand with three parade officials. The man on the left with the grey beard is a nod to author Dr. Seuss since the character looks much like the man in real life.

Catherine F. Olen

8. ★ Notice the motorcycle riding by the grandstand, what is this motorcycle used for in the city?
   a. Military
   b. Fire department
   c. Police
   d. Ice Cream man

> ### Did you know?
> Look down at the ground you will find footprints outside along just outside The High in the Sky Seuss Trolley Train Ride. Step into these footprints and listen for a special message from the Sneetches.

The High in the Sky Seuss Trolley Train Ride!

9. ★ Take a look at the sign outside The High in the Sky Seuss Trolley Train Ride. Which of these is *not* one of the colors of the train carts you see on the sign?
   a. Blue
   b. Purple
   c. Green
   d. Red

10. ★ As you enter the queue for The High in the Sky Seuss Trolley Train Ride, stop for a moment at the portrait of Mr. McBean. What is his first name?
    a. Arnold
    b. Jeremy
    c. Sydney
    d. Sylvester

11. ★ As you walk along the queue, read the story as you go. When the star belly sneetches had their frankfurter roast, where were the plain belly sneetches left?
    a. The dark of the beaches
    b. The caves of the mountains
    c. The rain and the cold
    d. The desert

12. ★ How much money was Sylvester McMonkey McBean charging for stars?
    a. $3.00
    b. $30.00
    c. $300.00
    d. .30¢

13. ★ When the Sneetches started come out on the machine with stars on their bellies, what did the Sneetches who already have star groan?
    a. "Great Cesar's ghost"
    b. "Oh no"
    c. "Good grief"
    d. "Holy moly"

14. ★ How much does Sylvester McMonkey McBean charge the Sneetches to remove their stars?
    a. $7.00
    b. $8.00
    c. $10.00
    d. $16.00

15. ★★ Find the sign to tell you where the story continues, where does it say to go?
    a. Downstairs
    b. Upstairs
    c. Out the exit
    d. Next door

> ### Did you know?
> As you walk up the stairs, notice the equipment in the center. Take a peek through the window and see a workman inside the door.

16. ★★ As you start your ride, you will enter the Circus McGurkus, according to your narrator this is the greatest show where?
    a. The city
    b. The country
    c. The earth
    d. The world

17. ★★★ As you circle the circus tent, look at the walrus at the center standing on three balls, 2 tennis and 3 of what other kind?
    a. Baseball
    b. Golf
    c. Football
    d. Ping pong

18. ★ As you go through the cavern with the sneetches, what color is the fish just below their cookout?
    a. Green
    b. Pink
    c. Yellow
    d. Black

19. ★★ As you exit the train, take a look around the ticket booth in the center of the load area. What time does the trolley leave for the desert of Zind?
    a. 3:51
    b. 2:50 ½
    c. 12:21
    d. 10:01

20. ★★ At 11:11, you will leave for the island of _____?
    a. Gwark
    b. Snark
    c. Olf
    d. Seuss

Did you know?

As you entered Island of Adventure, you undoubtedly missed a chance to see Sneetch Beach. Before you leave the theme park, be sure to walk to the edge of the lake and look across towards Seuss Landing. You will see the Sneetches have left their belongings on the beach to go on an adventure.

Dr. Seuss All the Books You Can Read

21. ★ As you enter the store, what famous Dr. Seuss character greets you in the middle of the room?
    a. Horton
    b. Cindy Lou Who
    c. The Cat in the Hat
    d. The Grinch

22. ★★ Look high above you and find the book to be read in what location?
    a. At the beach
    b. In bed
    c. At school
    d. While eating bread

> **Did you know?**
> Outside of this store, don't miss the topiary animals sitting and waiting for you to take pictures of them. Be sure to keep an eye out for The Cat in the Hat, Thing 1 and 2 or the Grinch. They may be waiting nearby also.

23. ★★ As you continue your stroll through Seuss Landing, you will come to the Street of the Lifted Lorax. Find the bare patch of dirt with several tree stumps. What is the name of these trees?
    a. Puffy
    b. Fingerlings
    c. Truffulas
    d. Hortonians

24. ★ High above, you will find the home of the Once-ler. What color is the sign with his name?
    a. Green
    b. Red
    c. Yellow
    d. White

> **Did you know?**
> Be sure to get your picture with the Lorax before continuing with your day in Seuss Landing.

Catherine F. Olen

The Cat in the Hat

> **Did you know?**
> Before you strap into your ride on The Cat in the Hat, be warned.... This ride spins and is quite dizzying for those with motion sickness.

25. ★★ As you come to The Cat in The Hat, take a look at what holds the sign up. What time does the blue clock read?
    a. 5:39
    b. 4:39
    c. 6:39
    d. 7:39

26. ★★ What food item do you see waving at the top of the stack of things for The Cat in the Hat sign?
    a. Pie
    b. Doughnut
    c. Candy apple
    d. Cake

27. ★ As you enter your ride vehicle, what piece of furniture makes up this vehicle?
    a. Bed
    b. Dining room set
    c. Couch
    d. Lounge chairs

28. ★★★ Mother is about to leave, take a quick look at her grocery list. What is the fourth item on her list?
    a. Cheese
    b. Milk
    c. Bread
    d. Polish

29. ★★ As you see the Cat in the Hat arrive at the front door, how many books are there on the table next to the door?
    a. Three
    b. Two
    c. Four
    d. Twelve

30. ★★ Watch the shadow of the cat balancing the fish bowl. What item is he using to balance the bowl?
    a. Cane
    b. Rake
    c. Umbrella
    d. Mop

31. ★★ How many books do you see the cat balancing in his left hand as you pass by?
    a. Five
    b. Six
    c. Ten
    d. Three

32. ★ As you come down the hall, what household item do you see the fish inside of?
    a. Coffee pot
    b. Flower vase
    c. Water glass
    d. Teapot

33. ★ Find Thing 1 playing with the television, what snack food do you see resting next to him?
    a. Peanuts
    b. Popcorn
    c. Ice cream
    d. Chips

34. ★★ What item of clothing is attached to the kite string above your head as you pass by the flying kite?
    a. A hat
    b. Pants
    c. A dress
    d. A coat

35. ★★ As you ride through the bathroom, what characters picture do you see on the toilet paper thrown around the room?
    a. Thing 1 and 2
    b. The Cat in the Hat
    c. Horton
    d. Dr. Seuss

36. ★ Be careful as Thing 1 and 2 throw what item down the stairs at you?
    a. Anvil
    b. Piano
    c. Safe
    d. Bed

37. ★ What item is used to capture Thing 1 and 2?
    a. A box
    b. Tongs
    c. A net
    d. A mousetrap

---

38. ★ As you exit the Cat in the Hat through Cat's, Hat's & Things, find the nest titled, Horton Hatches the Egg. According to the story, what was wrong with the bird's legs?
    a. Cramps
    b. Sprains
    c. Lumps
    d. Kinks

39. ★ What color is the polka dot egg in the nest?
    a. White
    b. Red
    c. Blue
    d. Green

One Fish, Two Fish, Red Fish, Blue Fish

40. ★ What color are the letters spelling out One Fish, Two Fish, Red Fish Blue Fish on the sign leading to this attraction?
    a. Blue
    b. Purple
    c. Green
    d. Yellow

41. ★ How many ride vehicles do you see for One Fish, Two Fish, Red Fish, Blue Fish?
    a. 15
    b. 12
    c. 10
    d. 20

42. ★★ Nearby, you will find McElligot's pool. According to the story, how long was Marco fishing without a single bite?
    a. 3 hours
    b. 3 days
    c. 2 hours
    d. 24 hours

The Great Universal Studios Orlando Scavenger Hunt

If I Ran the Zoo

43. ★★ As you look over the cages stacked up at the entrance of If I Ran the Zoo, notice the sign for Wild Animals on the Tiger cage has been scratched out. What has been written to replace this?
    a. Silly baby
    b. Big hairy
    c. Brand new
    d. Old fashioned

44. ★ Stop for a moment to read the code of conduct for Zoo Keeper. Why must you look after the adults?
    a. They cause trouble
    b. They get lost
    c. They scare the children
    d. They can't be trusted

45. ★ At the end of the code of conduct, be sure to say what?
    a. Bye
    b. Oh my
    c. Hi
    d. Sky high

46. ★ At the end of the hedge you will find a purple wall with several peek holes. What island did the zoo keeper travel too?
    a. Ka-troo
    b. A-choo
    c. Kanga-roo
    d. Dinga-do

47. ★★ As you look along the green hedge you will find a small area with a note about a shy boy. What must you be good at to meet him?
    a. Tickling toes
    b. Blowing your nose
    c. Counting crows
    d. Saying hello to Moe

48. ★ Find the peek hole that encourages you to insert your camera, how much will this cost you?
    a. Ten dollars
    b. 1 Gazillion
    c. Ten billion
    d. Free

49. ★★ In a cave in Katroom lives a beast called a what? Find the name near the cave you can crawl through.
    a. Catch
    b. Natch
    c. Stash
    d. Batch

50. ★ As you walk through the water park, stop to read the sign about catching dangerous animals. With what item is it too dangerous to catch them with?
    a. A butterfly net
    b. A rope made from vines
    c. Your bare hands
    d. Your favorite scarf

51. ★★ Find the yellow sign in the water park, what are they giving away for free?
    a. Air
    b. Water
    c. Sunshine
    d. Fun

52. ★ Read the sign on the door with two bells, what is unusual about the lady who lives there?
    a. She has a long neck
    b. She has small toes
    c. She owns 72 cats
    d. She loves little children

53. ★★★ Come to the sign for McGrew's Zoo. How many lightbulbs light up this sign?
    a. 136
    b. 144
    c. 124
    d. 134

Did you know?

Don't miss an opportunity to ride the cow since he roams free inside the zoo. This is a wonderful photo opportunity for the whole family.

The Great Universal Studios Orlando Scavenger Hunt

54. ★★ What special game can you play with McGrew's friend Joe?
    a. Hopscotch
    b. Jump rope
    c. Tic Tac Toe
    d. Checkers

55. ★ Find the animal taking a bath. What color is the bar of soap resting on the tub?
    a. Blue
    b. Green
    c. Yellow
    d. Pink

56. ★ How long has this animal been in the bath tub according to the note left for you?
    a. Two weeks Friday
    b. Since last Tuesday
    c. Last month
    d. Ten days

57. ★ What bath time toy do you see sitting on the shelf near the bathtub?
    a. Rubber duck
    b. Beach ball
    c. Sailboat
    d. Rubber octopus

58. ★ Find the quarantine sign for Mulli, what sort of area is he from originally?
    a. Icy polar ice caps
    b. Bottom of the ocean
    c. Blistering sand of the desert
    d. Somewhere no one has ever been

Did you know?

As you finish your time in Seuss Landing, be sure to find the Green Egg's and Ham building. This icon of Dr. Seuss includes green eggs used as umbrellas and high above, the large green ham.

You have finished your tour of Universal Studios Florida and Universal Islands of Adventure; I hope you have found many exciting new adventures and rediscovered old favorites while reading the pages of The Great Universal Studios Orlando Scavenger Hunt.

It has been a pleasure to write this book as the Universal theme parks have been a favorite of mine for almost thirty years. One of my passions is to show others the hidden wonders throughout every theme park I visit, and I hope you found this book has added to your pleasure during your visits to Universal Studios Orlando resort.

Answer Key

Universal Studios Orlando

Production Central

Shrek 4-D

1. C – Fairy tale
2. D – The crusher
3. C – Kneecaps
4. A – Torture
5. B – Lancelot
6. D – Magic mirror
7. C – Mr. Sniffles
8. A – *Cat on a Hot Tin Roof*
9. C - Enchanted
10. A – Fiona
11. B – 11 seconds
12. C – 7 Candy cane lane
13. A – Drunkenly call old girlfriends' hour
14. C – A lot of dough
15. D – Coming soon
16. B – Dragon

17. C – Crocodile
18. A – Honeymoon Hotel
19. B – Troll bridge
20. D – Spring time!

Despicable Me Minion Mayhem

21. D – 3 feet
22. A – Peanut
23. A – Leopold
24. C – Felonius
25. C – Werewolf
26. B – 41
27. A – Bird
28. D – Octavia
29. B – Happy faces
30. D – Sock puppet
31. C – 3 weeks
32. D – The person wearing them
33. A – A fork
34. D – Dynamite
35. C – Banana
36. B – A cactus
37. C – Fly swatter
38. A – Yellow
39. D – Anti-gravity
40. C – Gru doll

Universal Studios Classic Monster's Cafe

41. B – Dracula
42. C – Bone chilling
43. D – 1921
44. A – It's upside down
45. C – Elsa Lanchester

Transformers™ the Ride-3D

46. B – 28 feet
47. A – Cybertronian
48. D – Security
49. C – Hero recruitment officer
50. D – Species
51. B – Bumblebee
52. A – Rampage
53. C – War
54. B – The AllSpark
55. D – A churro
56. C – Insects
57. A – Devastator
58. C – Beg for mercy
59. B – Bumblebee
60. D – Freedom fighters
61. D – Yellow

New York Street

Race Through New York Starring Jimmy Fallon

1. B – Bill Paxton
2. C – The Metropolis Tribune
3. D – Twister Cola
4. C – 1955
5. A – *This Could Be the Start of Something*
6. D – Carnac
7. A – Conan O'Brien
8. B – Xylophone
9. D – 40
10. A – Applause
11. D – Central Park
12. A – The Shadow and The Light
13. D – Music

Catherine F. Olen

14. B – Polish
15. C – Fine jewelry
16. B – *Thoroughly Modern Millie*
17. A – 1939

The Revenge of the Mummy

18. D – Paradise
19. A – Modern items
20. B – Riches
21. D – Scarab beetles
22. B – Cup of coffee
23. C – Getting latte
24. B – Wagon
25. A – Coleman's
26. D – 15¢
27. D – *Funny Face*
28. B – The Lady of Shalott
29. A – Rolls
30. B – $2.00
31. C – Max
32. D – 1720
33. B – Furniture
34. C – 35
35. A – *The Black Cat*
36. D – Gold
37. B – Coney Island
38. C – Singer
39. B – Governor Earl Long
40. A – No standing
41. A – Passport
42. D – The Canary Islands
43. B – Janis Paige
44. C – Shamrocks
45. B – Clarinet

The Great Universal Studios Orlando Scavenger Hunt

46. D – Military Miniatures
47. A – Snooker
48. C – Silver Cup
49. B – Baseball

San Francisco

1. B - .79¢
2. C – Irish moss
3. A – Alfred Klein
4. D – Hiccups
5. C - Asthma
6. A – Catnip
7. D – $100.00
8. B – Lew Wasserman
9. A – 17

Richter's Burger Co.

10. B – $24.60
11. D – Alex and the Aftershocks

Fast & Furious: Supercharged

12. A – Machine operator
13. B – Problems
14. D – Tarantino's
15. B – Marie
16. C – OUTATIME
17. A – Hotel Californian
18. D – Sullivan's Garage
19. C – 6:45
20. B – Carpentry
21. D – 2007
22. A – Sweetwater, TN
23. B – Spitting

24. A – Tej
25. B – 555-9782
26. D – *Here's to Swimmin' with Bow Legged Women*

The Wizarding World of Harry Potter™ - Diagon Alley™

The Knight Bus

1. A – Dre Head
2. C – Green and yellow

Hogwarts Express – King's Cross Station

3. A – 9
4. B – 10:47
5. D – On time
6. B – On time
7. B – A stroller
8. A – 5972
9. B – Dementors
10. C – The food trolley
11. D – A skull
12. B – Dementor!
13. C – Chocolate frog
14. A – Hagrid
15. C – An empty compartment
16. A – A Hippogriff
17. A – Satyrs
18. D – Fireworks display
19. C – Licorice
20. A – The Knight Bus
21. C – Mad Eye Moody

Quality Quidditch™ Supplies

22. B – Firebolt
23. D – Wax
24. D – Chudley Cannons

Weasleys' Wizard Wheezes

25. B - Screaming Yo-Yo
26. A – Dolores Umbridge
27. C – Mayhem
28. A – Rabbit
29. D – Elephant
30. B – Sitars
31. C – Slugs
32. D – Flies
33. A – The golden snitch
34. C – 39 years
35. B – Swish
36. C – Frog
37. D – House elves
38. A – Wednesday
39. D – A telephone
40. B – Hamburger
41. C – Meat joints
42. A – King George V
43. C – Wigs

The Leaky Cauldron

44. B – Mutton tongue stew
45. B – Crispy bat wings
46. D – The witching hour
47. C – Magic
48. A – Eels

49. D – 7
50. C – 14

Flourish and Blotts Booksellers

51. A – 1454
52. A – Spells
53. C – Shredded paper
54. B – Pagan
55. D – Goat
56. B - Broadsheet

Madam Malkin's Robes for All Occasions

57. B – Hermione's ball gown

Mr. Mulpeppers Apothecary

58. B – 1106
59. C – Spleen
60. D – 400
61. C – Flying

Florean Fortescue's Ice Cream Parlor

62. A – Ambrosia
63. D – Lavender

Harry Potter and the Escape from Gringotts™

64. D – Dragon guarded
65. C – Money
66. B – The death of Albus Dumbledore
67. C – Transylvania
68. A – Weasleys' Wildfire Whiz-bangs
69. D – A magnifying glass
70. B – Bellatrix LeStrange

71. B – Horcrux
72. D – Aguamenti
73. C – Muggle born
74. D – Formals

Ollivanders™

75. A – 382 BC
76. C – Test-fly
77. C - Hippogriff tailfeather
78. A - The wand chooses the wizard
79. D - Never leave it in your back pocket
80. B – Shave N Save

Magical Menagerie

81. B – Hippopotamus
82. C – Snail
83. D – Luna Lovegood
84. B – Superlative Rat Tonic
85. A – Dancing Doxy
86. B – Magical mess remover
87. A – Hags
88. D – Ringworm
89. C – 1100
90. B – Green
91. C – Horned Slugs
92. A – Scarab beetle

Knockturn Alley

93. D – Bats
94. A – Web weavers
95. C – Un-tame
96. C – Mesmerizing
97. B – Witch

98. D – Confounded
99. A – Pawn broker

Borgin and Burkes™

100. B – Nineteen
101. C – Troll foot
102. D – Flesh-eating slug
103. C – House elf

World Expo

Men in Black™: Alien Attack

1. A – Roswell
2. B – Oxygen free zone
3. D – Folgers
4. C – Multipeds who sing and move well
5. B – Paradiso IV
6. A – Aliens make better coffee
7. D – Not for human consumption
8. C – Dinosaur
9. B – 1987

Springfield: Home of the Simpsons

1. A – The nuclear power plant
2. D – Bi monthly Sci-Fi Con
3. B – 9
4. C - #1DOOFUS
5. C – Drunky

Fast Food Blvd

6. D – Dead Lobster
7. B – Pandas
8. A – Face Smasher 6

9. B – Mr. Teeny
10. D – Miss Hoover
11. A – Martin
12. D – Fallout Boy
13. A – Dr. Julius Hibbert
14. B – 254
15. C – 408

Moe's Tavern

16. A – Casanova
17. C – No. 7
18. D – Jailbird Gin
19. B – 1886
20. D – The B Sharps
21. C – The Flaming Moe
22. A – 13
23. C – Happiness
24. B – Day old beaks

The Kwik-E-Mart

25. D – Cheap
26. C – James Woods
27. A – Beach sand
28. B – Stuffing
29. C – 5 pounds
30. A – Baby Gerald
31. D – Milhouse
32. D – Jalapeno Raspberry
33. B - $2.00
34. C – Dingus
35. A – El Barto

Kang and Kodos' Twist 'N' Hurl

36. B – Before you go on it
37. A – 4

The Simpsons Ride

38. C – Rip-off
39. D – Unhappy teen employees
40. B – Shame and rejection
41. A – Probed
42. B – Cletus
43. C – Sherri and Terri
44. D – McBain
45. C – Paris Texan
46. B – Yard work
47. A – The Longest Daycare
48. D – Hans Moleman
49. D – A date with Moe
50. C – Tire yard
51. B – The Traumanator Coaster
52. A – Side show Robert
53. C – Stringy candy
54. D – Fried sugar
55. A – Krusty
56. D – Switch
57. B – Bellybutton
58. B – Mr. Burns
59. C – 45 minutes
60. A – Nelson
61. C – Chain reactions
62. D – Killer whale
63. D – Maggie
64. B – Her pacifier
65. C – You don't know where they've been

66. A – Kang and Kodos
67. B – Bart Simpson
68. C – Aaaagh, this hurts!
69. D – Smiling Joe Fission

Woody Woodpecker's KidZone
SpongeBob StorePants

1. B – Deep fried
2. D – 100
3. A – Snail
4. C – Walk the plank
5. D – 300%
6. B – Receipt

E.T. Adventure

7. C – 1982
8. A – Steven Spielberg
9. C – Bottanicus
10. D – Three million light years
11. B – Interplanetary passport

Fievel's Playland

12. B – July 4, 1892
13. A – 30 days
14. C – A penny
15. A – Cat. R. Waul gang
16. D – yellow
17. C – Dowling, Ohio
18. A – *The Life and Time of Wiley Burp*
19. B – Harmonika box
20. B – 1877
21. A – Dog

22. C – 8
23. D – Swimming

Woody Woodpecker's Nuthouse Coaster

24. D – Are you a crack pot?
25. A – You
26. C – Woody
27. B – 11

Curious George goes to Town

28. C – Monkey
29. A – Yellow
30. D – World's smartest
31. B – Postponed
32. A – Giraffe
33. A – Collect calls
34. C – Blue
35. D – Monkey sets animals loose
36. B – Bathtub
37. C – 555-1234
38. B – Wally Rus
39. D – .10¢
40. A – Horse

Hollywood

1. C – 440 N. Camden Dr.
2. D – 1939
3. C – Groceries
4. C – Pig
5. D – Half Spring Chicken

Universal Orlando's Horror Make-up Show

6. B – Pantages
7. A – Lon Chaney
8. B – 1935
9. A – 1982
10. C – Rubber cement
11. B – Faces
12. D – The Phantom of the Opera
13. C – Bela Lugosi
14. D – Master of suspense
15. A – Chucky
16. B – Esoteric Pictures

Mel's Diner

17. D – Chevy Bel Air
18. B – 1932

Schwab's Drug Store

19. C – .59¢
20. D – Hershey's syrup
21. A – Elizabeth Taylor
22. B – Clark Gable
23. D – 44 %
24. C – Talcum
25. A – .01¢
26. C – Food
27. B – 1929

Islands of Adventure

Port of Entry

1. A – HMS Turner
2. B – Snow shoes
3. C – Camera
4. B – Sitar
5. A – The karat
6. C – Chocolate
7. D – Pineapple
8. B – Coins
9. B – 1196
10. A – Moved closer to water
11. B – Professor Cariatun
12. D – Didgeridoo
13. D – Cats

Confisco Grill

14. B – Boris and Natasha
15. C – Primrose Yellow
16. A - Confiscated
17. C – Easter Island
18. B – Croissant Moon
19. A – Baking powder

Marvel Super Hero Island

The Incredible Hulk Coaster

1. A – General Thaddeus Ross
2. C – G14
3. D – Unstable
4. C – 3
5. B – Hostility
6. B – Human Torch

7. D – 12
8. C – Silver Surfer
9. D – Kingpin
10. B – Wilson Fisk
11. C – Green Goblin
12. A – Time Square
13. A – Billy Nosegoblin
14. D – Weak
15. B – Cardio training
16. D – Matt
17. B – Carnage
18. A – Wolverine

Doctor Doom's Fearfall

19. B – Latveria
20. D – World domination

The Amazing Adventures of Spiderman

21. B – 7–9 a.m.
22. A – J. Jonah Jameson
23. C – Mary Jane Watson
24. A – Nick Fury
25. D – John F. Kennedy
26. B – 23,972
27. D – Geneva
28. C – Squid-rollers
29. A – Croissant
30. B – Look it up in the dictionary
31. A – Assci characters
32. A – The leaning tower of Pisa
33. D – Safety first
34. C – The Statue of Liberty
35. B – Green Goblin

36. D – 4.5 million
37. A – That traitor Spiderman
38. A – Stan Lee
39. C – Don't pass
40. B – Trouble
41. D – Nice shades
42. C – Excelsior

Toon Lagoon

1. B – Broom Hilda
2. B – U.S.M.C.
3. A – Heart
4. C – Choir practice
5. D – Muenster
6. C – 8
7. B – A beer mug
8. C – Skunk
9. A – Vulture
10. C – Claude Clay

Blondies: Home of the Dagwood

11. D – Peanut butter
12. B – Authority
13. C – Color
14. A – Spoon

Dudley Do-right's Ripsaw Falls®

15. D – Attorney
16. B – A rose
17. C – Admit one
18. A – Grizzly
19. A – A bird
20. B – Broom closet

21. D – Snidely Whiplash
22. C – Minnesota
23. B – Antlers
24. D – Fiend
25. A – Canoe
26. C – Wontyabe mine
27. A – Horse
28. B – His train of thought
29. A – Accidents
30. D – Real logs
31. C – 0%
32. B – Prison
33. D – Beaver
34. B – Dog
35. B – Award ceremony

Comic Strip Café

36. A – Vowels
37. C – He lacked dimension
38. D – The Cat in the Hat
39. C – Woody Woodpecker

Popeye and Bluto's Bilge-Rat Barges

40. B – Sweet Pea
41. D – Gangplank
42. A – Poison
43. C – Olive Oyl
44. A – Mermaid calling
45. C – 327
46. D – Pull the rope
47. A – Anchors
48. D – Brute of the year
49. B – First dollar stolen

50. C – Grab a bar of soap
51. A – He's a good friend
52. D – Tide
53. B – Patcheye the Pirate
54. C – Salty
55. B – High seas
56. A – Lumber Jack Love
57. D – Bombs
58. C – Landlubber
59. C - Burgers
60. B – Olive Oyl
61. A - Octopus
62. C – S.S. Stinker
63. A – Eight
64. C – Mr. Peabody

Skull Island: Reign of Kong

1. B – Tea
2. C – Eighth Wonder
3. D – Worm
4. C – October 23, 1929
5. A – Investigate native sightings
6. A – Jared
7. C – Replacement supplies
8. B – Kong
9. D – Bats
10. C – Flare gun
11. A – Tyrannosaurus Rex
12. D – Spirits

The Great Universal Studios Orlando Scavenger Hunt

Jurassic Park
Jurassic Park River Adventure

1. B – Eating
2. D – Time
3. C – Diloposarus
4. C – 13
5. D – Be alert
6. A – Three-horn face

Jurassic Park Discovery Center

7. B – L-Lysine
8. C – Tranquilizer gun
9. A – Millipore
10. D – Gas wash

Camp Jurassic

11. B – Rock climbing

The Wizarding World of Harry Potter™ - Hogsmeade

1. B – 1867
2. D – Monocle
3. A – Puking Pastilles
4. D – Sweets

Honeydukes™

5. B – 34
6. D – Ice
7. D – Snakes
8. B – Halloween
9. A – 50.00
10. A – 24 February

Three Broomsticks™

11. B – 36

Hog's Head™ Pub

12. A – Steak and Kidney Pudding
13. A – The witching hour
14. C – 5
15. B – Your head
16. D – Winter
17. D - Snakeweed
18. B – Owls

Dervish and Banges™

19. C – Bite you
20. B – Deodorant
21. D – Dominic Maestro
22. A – Owl breeds
23. D- Cast a security spell

Owl Post

24. C – Witches hat
25. A – Permission form
26. C - Crystal

Gladrags Wizardwear

27. B – A cat
28. A – Out fitting

Scrivenshaft's Finest Parchment, Ink and Quills

29. D – Singer

Madam Puddifoot's

30. C – Heart
31. A – 16
32. B – Sunflowers
33. C – 11

Ceridwen's Cauldrons

34. D – 17

Tomes and Scrolls Specialist Bookshop

35. B – 1768
36. A – Meandering with Mummies
37. C – Luxos Karuzos
38. D – Garden
39. C – Fair fortune
40. B – Royal

Flight of the Hippogriff™

41. D – Pumpkins
42. A – The forest is forbidden to all students
43. C – Sirius Black
44. B – Norwegian Ridgeback

Ollivanders™

45. A – 382 BC
46. A – The wand chooses the wizard
47. D – Hippogriff tail feather
48. C – Never store it in your back pocket

Harry Potter and the Forbidden Journey™

49. D – Erised
50. C – Neville
51. A – A scroll
52. D – Gryffindor
53. A – The chapel
54. A – 1709
55. D – Salazar Slytherin
56. B – The dark side
57. C – Lord Voldemort
58. D – What is easy
59. A – A few short hours
60. D – Cloak of invisibility
61. B – It's fascinating
62. C – See a game of Quidditch
63. D – It starts snowing
64. B – Relive your worst memories
65. A – Happy memory
66. B – Dragon
67. C – Apples
68. D – Backgammon
69. A – Goblin
70. C – Wizard
71. B – Hermione
72. D – A metal chain and collar
73. A – The Whomping Willow
74. C – The Great Hall
75. D – Lord Voldemort

The Lost Continent

Poseidon's Fury: Escape from the Lost City

1. B – Trident
2. C – Octopus

The Great Universal Studios Orlando Scavenger Hunt

3. A – 2000 years
4. B – Priests of the Inner Circle
5. D – The chamber of sacrifice
6. C – Professor Baxter
7. A – Darkanon
8. A – Poseidon's trident
9. B – Your destiny
10. D – Spiderman
11. C – The Goddess
12. D – Locking spell impervious to magic
13. B – Safe passage deeper into the temple
14. A – Octopus
15. B – A thousand years ago

Seuss Landing

1. D – Sour gooseberry jam
2. A – Six
3. B – Zamp

Mulberry Street Store, Gizmo's, Gadgets, Goodies Galore

4. C – Giraffe
5. A – 70500 zillion
6. D – 472
7. B – 5:55
8. C – Police

The High in The Sky Seuss Trolley Train Ride!

9. B – Purple
10. D – Sylvester
11. A – The dark of the beaches
12. A – $3.00
13. C – "Good grief"

14. C – $10.00
15. B – Upstairs
16. D – The world
17. B – Golf
18. A – Green
19. C – 12:21
20. A – Gwark

Dr. Seuss All the Books You Can Read

21. D – The Grinch
22. B – In bed
23. C – Truffulas
24. A - Green

The Cat in the Hat

25. B – 4:39
26. D – Cake
27. C – Couch
28. A – Cheese
29. A – Three
30. C – Umbrella
31. B – Six
32. D – Teapot
33. B – Popcorn
34. C – A dress
35. A – Thing 1 and 2
36. B – Piano
37. C – A net
38. D – Kinks
39. B – Red

One Fish, Two Fish, Red Fish, Blue Fish

40. D – Yellow
41. B – 12
42. A – 3 hours

If I Ran the Zoo

43. D – Old fashioned
44. B – They get lost
45. C – Hi
46. A – Ka-troo
47. A – Tickling toes
48. D – Free
49. B – Natch
50. C – Your bare hands
51. B – Water
52. A – She has a long neck
53. D – 134
54. C – Tic Tac Toe
55. D – Pink
56. B – Since last Tuesday
57. A – Rubber duck
58. C – Blistering sand of the desert

www.ingramcontent.com/pod-product-compliance
Lightning Source LLC
Chambersburg PA
CBHW071159070526
44584CB00019B/2852